THE CASE
AGAINST
PRIVATE
AVIATION

THE CASE
AGAINST
PRIVATE
AVIATION

by Donald Bain

COWLES BOOK COMPANY, INC.

NEW YORK

DEDICATION

To many people, but especially to R. H. "Red" Sutherland, who knows and loves aviation and has shared both with me, and to my editor, Bob Meskill, who understands what portions of enthusiasm and journalism blend to achieve a proper brew.

And most of all, this book is dedicated to the millions of airline passengers who have the right to some assurance that reasonable men are using their knowledge and position to better the aviation environment.

There is hereby recognized and declared to exist in behalf of any citizen of the United States a public right of freedom of transit in air commerce through the navigable air space of the United States.

Section 104
Federal Aviation Act of 1958

That action is best which procures the greatest happiness for the greatest numbers.

Francis Hutcheson
Inquiry Concerning Moral Good and Evil . . . Section 3

CONTENTS

THE CASE
AGAINST
PRIVATE
AVIATION

CHAPTER ONE

Death in the Skies

On March 9, 1967, two airplanes collided over Urbana, Ohio. One of the aircraft was a TWA commercial DC-9 jet carrying twenty-one passengers and a crew of four. The other was a twin-engine Beechcraft Baron, one of many types of aircraft classified in the category of general or private aviation. It carried one man, its pilot.

Both planes crashed to the ground after impact.

There were no survivors.

The following chronological account of the events leading to the Urbana tragedy will allow the reader to formulate his own conclusions as to where the fault in the accident should be placed. He will be left with two alternatives: Was the pilot of the TWA passenger jet at fault for failing to maintain an adequate lookout for other planes in the area? Or was the pilot of the Beechcraft at fault for being in the area in the first place? If the latter is determined by the reader, then the system that allowed the smaller plane to operate as it did must also share in the blame.

Cyrus Burgstahler, 54, an experienced pilot with 4,074 flying hours, taxied the Beechcraft Baron B-55 to the end of the runway at Detroit City Airport. His high number of accumulated flying hours, coupled with the fact that he held a full instrument rating, the same type of rating for all-weather flying as held by airline pilots, ranked Burgstahler high on the scale of experience and proficiency for non-airline pilots.

The weather in Detroit that morning was not good enough for pilots to operate by visual flight rules (VFR), those rules under which a pilot flies only by his own visual references and without control of anyone on the ground. Of course, bad weather would seldom pose a problem for an instrument-rated pilot like Burgstahler. He could simply request an instrument clearance. But, at the time of his flight, he had another choice. Under existing regulations, he could request a *special* visual flight rules (SVFR) clearance. This type of clearance was available to private pilots when weather minimums were below those necessary for a regular visual clearance, but above those that would make instrument flight mandatory. In a word, it was a legal loophole under which non-instrument-rated private pilots could fly on marginal days. Burgstahler had his choice of clearances and chose the easier alternative. He chose to depart Detroit and fly his route under the special visual flight rules clearance, which necessitated nothing more than asking for that clearance. He wasn't required to file any flight plan; his intended destination and route of flight would be known only to him. He was not required to inform anyone of his plans.

He advanced the throttles, and soon the forty-five-hundred-pound, sixty-thousand-dollar aircraft was rolling down the runway at Detroit. It was airborne at 11:01 eastern standard time.

Burgstahler headed south toward Springfield, Ohio. This was a business trip; he'd made the same flight just seven days previous. He was rested, having retired at eleven o'clock the night before. It was all very routine.

Twenty-four minutes after the Beechcraft lifted off at

Detroit City Airport, TWA Flight 553 completed its takeoff roll at Greater Pittsburgh Airport. It lifted off the ground, cleared the Pittsburgh area, and proceeded southwest toward its next destination, Dayton, Ohio. Flight 553 was what the trade called a puddle jumper. It originated in New York in the morning and terminated in Chicago, with stops at Harrisburg, Pittsburgh, and Dayton in between.

At the controls of Flight 553 was Captain Karl Kohlsaat, 39, a TWA pilot since 1956. He had 9,832 hours of flying time behind him and was fully qualified to command the DC-9, one of the newer twin-engine, short-haul jets being utilized by the airlines.

Seated next to Captain Kohlsaat in the cockpit was First Officer Donald Binder, 29, with TWA since 1965 and checked out on the DC-9.

Flight 553 reached its assigned cruising altitude of Flight Level 200 (twenty thousand feet) and maintained that altitude until it approached the Dayton Municipal Airport area. Captain Kohlsaat was advised by the Dayton Control Center to descend to five thousand feet. He was also advised that the radar tracking his flight, accomplished up to that point by the Indianapolis Ground Control Center, would be transferred to the Dayton area control facility. Captain Kohlsaat first spoke with Dayton at 11:52:36. At that time, the flight was approximately eight miles northeast of Urbana, Ohio.

At 11:53:22, Dayton Control cleared Captain Kohlsaat to descend from five thousand to three thousand feet and to make a left turn to a heading of 230 degrees, or almost precisely south-southwest.

"Roger," Kohlsaat responded, indicating his understanding of and compliance with the order.

Almost at the same moment as Captain Kohlsaat was talking with Dayton Control, Cyrus Burgstahler made his only radio contact in the Dayton area. He called Springfield Aviation,

Inc., at the Springfield Airport, and requested a courtesy car upon his arrival. He informed them he'd be landing soon. His call was completed at approximately 11:53:30.

Burgstahler had no sooner completed his call to Springfield than the air traffic controller at Dayton responsible for tracking Flight 553 on radar first noticed a strange blip on his radar screen. That blip, or spot on the screen, was made by Burgstahler's Beechcraft as it entered the Dayton area. It came as a total surprise to the controller on the ground. Had Burgstahler filed a flight plan, Dayton would have been notified of his intended route of flight through that area.

"TWA 553," the Dayton controller said into his microphone.

"Roger," Kohlsaat answered.

"Traffic at twelve-thirty, one mile, southbound, slow moving." The Dayton controller completed this message at 11:53:35.

"Roger," Captain Kohlsaat responded one second later, at 11:53:36.

Burgstahler proceeded on his southerly flight path through the Dayton control area. Captain Kohlsaat and First Officer Binder were already involved in the cockpit procedures necessary to prepare for a landing at Dayton. Throttle settings were continuously adjusted for speed control, path of flight was constantly monitored and corrected to insure a proper approach heading, altitude was checked for accuracy in the instrument landing approach pattern, and an extensive pre-landing checklist was run through by both cockpit crew members.

"Ready on the checklist, Cap'n," Binder said at 11:53:46.

Four seconds later—11:53:50—the DC-9 and the Beechcraft collided. The smaller plane disintegrated on impact. The larger DC-9, according to the only witness on the ground, hovered for a moment. Then its left wing dipped down, the angle of bank increasing until the wings no longer provided the needed lift for the aircraft. It fell sharply to the snow-covered ground, nose down.

The wreckage of the two aircraft was found scattered over an area approximately 2.3 miles long and one-half mile wide. The fatality toll was as would be expected. Midair collisions seldom leave survivors.

The accident set into motion an elaborate and thorough investigation by the Bureau of Aviation Safety, formerly a part of the Civil Aeronautics Board (CAB) and more recently placed under the newly formed National Transportation Safety Board (NTSB).

The investigation of any fatal civil air accident is impressive in its scope as well as in its attention to detail. Whole teams of experts converge on the accident scene. The damaged aircraft are pieced together as completely as possible. Flight recorders, the devices on commercial airliners that record the movements of the aircraft in flight, are retrieved and analyzed. Human-factors experts grapple with the human elements that might have contributed to the accident. Air traffic control authorities scrutinize the second-by-second ground monitoring of the aircraft. And weathermen search for meaningful meteorological factors.

Seventeen months after the Urbana accident, the NTSB issued its findings as to the probable cause of the accident. Such determinations are not to fix blame, but to apply knowledge gained to the prevention of future accidents of a similar nature. There are, of course, other ramifications to an NTSB declaration of probable cause in a civil aviation accident. All special interest groups representing the factions involved in the accident eagerly await the finger of blame to be pointed by the NTSB. These groups include: manufacturers of the aircraft, pilots' associations, air traffic control associations, the airline itself, and, in a case like Urbana, industrial trade groups representing general and private aviation. All anxiously await the decision and stand ready to defend their special interests in the event the decision puts them in a momentary bad light.

On August 1, 1968, the NTSB released its official report.

"The board determines the probable cause of this accident was the failure of the DC-9 crew to see and avoid the Beech-craft."

Case closed.

But should it have been?

The NTSB's investigation and its resulting decision were based upon the prevailing rule of "see and be seen." Under this time-honored rule of flying, each pilot of an aircraft has the distinct responsibility to see and avoid other aircraft sharing his air space. This rule holds regardless of whether he is under the control of a ground radar station. It holds despite the entrance of the jet age into what was once a fly-by-the-seat-of-your-pants aviation environment. Seeing and avoiding other aircraft prevails as the rule in every corner of the nation, from the smallest town to the largest city, including those served by New York's Kennedy, LaGuardia, and Newark airports, Chicago's O'Hare, and Washington's National and Dulles. It is a holdover from another era, and is defended by general and private aviation as adamantly as they defend the rights granted *all* citizens to *all* airspace by the Federal Aviation Act of 1958.

With see-and-be-seen the rule, the NTSB's findings in the Urbana accident are understandable. But a much larger question emerges from that investigation. Simply stated, it asks whether the needs and capabilities of today's aviation environment must continue to be met under the thinking of another era in which flying by the seat of one's pants was adequate to insure a reasonable level of safety. When applied specifically to Urbana, the question can be enlarged. Should many airline passengers be jeopardized for the rights of a few? Should the pilots who command today's and to-morrow's highly sophisticated and swift jet aircraft, each responsible for many passengers, also be forced to maintain a vigilance for small, private planes flying under uncontrolled visual flight rules while they, the airline pilots, operate under strict and continuous ground control? Or, perhaps more important, are they *able* to see and avoid these other aircraft?

The experts at the National Transportation Safety Board are aware of the larger problems. They further commented in their Urbana findings, "Contributing to this cause [Urbana] were physiological and environmental conditions and the excessive speed of the DC-9 which reduced visual detection capabilities under the air traffic control system which was not designed or equipped to separate a mixture of controlled and uncontrolled traffic." (At the time of the collision, the DC-9 had been exceeding a recently imposed speed limit on aircraft arriving at airports. The regulation, Part 91.85 of the Federal Air Regulations [FAR], prohibits an arriving aircraft from exceeding 288 miles per hour within thirty miles of the destination airport and when under ten thousand feet of altitude. TWA Flight 553 was found to have been descending at approximately 370 miles per hour. This regulation was due, in part, to pressure from private aviation lobbying interests. The speed limit was imposed purely to lessen the chance of a jet aircraft running into a private plane. Speeds in excess of the limit are in no way dangerous in themselves and, according to some veteran pilots, such speed controls can contribute to unsafe handling of large jet aircraft at lower altitudes.)

The NTSB also said in its findings, "The lack of positive control over aircraft operations conducted in terminal areas under the present day traffic control system is not satisfactory. Had the Beechcraft been under control of an air traffic controller the accident could have been avoided because the controller could have arranged to sequence the two aircraft in such a manner as to avoid any converging of their flight paths."

The NTSB went on to say, "The board recognizes that the operation of high speed aircraft with accelerated closure rates; frequent but necessary diversion of attention to cockpit duties; and current conspicuity problems, places a difficult burden upon flight crews."

Referring directly to the Urbana findings, it said, "During descent from cruising altitude in preparation for landing at Dayton, the cockpit crew workload of the DC-9 flight crew would probably have been as high or higher than at any other phase of the flight. The crew would have been performing such functions as monitoring air traffic control transmissions, making aircraft heading and speed changes, accomplishing checklist items and looking out for other traffic in the area. The board also recognizes that the 'see and be seen' concept is not a practical solution to the problems of high-speed closure rates which, on certain occasions, confront the crews of modern aircraft. The situation as it now exists is one in which ATC [air traffic control] cannot assure an appropriate level of safety between 'known' and 'unknown' traffic operations, nor can the pilots of the high-speed modern aircraft safely operate these aircraft in accordance with 'see and be seen' VFR [visual flight rules] right-of-way rules in the short period of time available to them for detection and corrective action."

The pilot of the TWA DC-9, Captain Kohlsaat, was officially found at fault for not seeing and avoiding the Beechcraft flown by Burgstahler. Spokesmen for private and general aviation interest agreed with the findings.

There are those who disagree, including this writer. The concept of see-and-be-seen as applied to aviation safety today is but one area into which this book will delve. There are many other areas. Each is vitally important to every man, woman, and child who takes part in the jet age as a paying passenger on the nation's commercial airlines.

The stakes of aviation safety are high, and grow higher each year. The increase in air travel is testimony to both an affluent economy and a booming aviation industry. In 1926, only 5,782 people paid their fares and boarded airplanes as passengers. By 1942, that number had grown to 4,060,545. In 1958, 56 million airline passengers were counted. The count went up to 130 million in 1967; 1968 saw the figure rise to 150 million. And industry statisticians forecast that the number of airline passengers will triple by 1979. As many as 1 million passengers a day will be served by the nation's scheduled commercial airlines. Kennedy Airport alone is expected to be handling 40 million passengers a year by 1980. The total number of all airline passengers should reach somewhere over 445 million in that same year.

The most pressing need for these millions of airline passengers is their safety while flying. The insurance of this safety will depend basically on three segments of what is termed the *aviation safety systems concept.* These three segments are the federal government and its agencies responsible for aviation safety, the nation's scheduled air carriers, more commonly known as the airlines, and that sprawling and rapidly growing segment known as general aviation into which all non-airline aircraft and operations are lumped. Within the general aviation category are included corporate aircraft and operations, industrial aircraft and operations (fire fighting, pipeline inspection, crop dusting, and so on), and private aviation—the pleasure-flying group. According to a Federal Aviation Administration (FAA) study released in February, 1969, pleasure flying accounted for the greatest number of general aviation flying hours in 1967. The same held true in 1968.

The federal government and its agencies must provide a workable system in which the other two segments of the safety systems chain—the airlines and general aviation—can operate safely. A sterling performance by one or even two segments is not effective without a like performance from the third safety partner.

To date, only one of the three partners in safety has performed with any accomplishment. That single segment is the commercial airlines. The safety record achieved by the nation's scheduled commercial airlines is extremely impressive. As much as one million dollars is spent by the airlines on each new jet aircraft for safety-oriented equipment alone.

Crews are trained and retrained beyond the minimum standards stipulated by the FAA. Maintenance programs for airline aircraft are extensive and thorough.

In fact, were aviation safety the airlines' alone to insure, the prognosis would be good. Perhaps excellent.

But in the systems concept of safety, in which all elements must contribute equally, aviation safety becomes less sure as each year comes and goes. The needed cooperation and contributions to the system from the federal government and general and/or private aviation have not been forthcoming. In fact, both these segments of the system have proved themselves detrimental to an improved air safety system. In some ways, they have managed this independently of each other. In others, they have become partners in hindering aviation safety, perhaps inadvertently so but partners nonetheless.

There are many gauges by which air safety can be judged for its effectiveness. One is the number of near-miss incidents occurring in our skies.

A near-miss is simply what the term indicates: a situation in which two aircraft are closer to each other in flight than deemed safe. Some come closer than others. Some demand sudden evasive action on the part of one or both pilots. Some happen so quickly that only chance intervenes and keeps the two aircraft from coming together in flight.

Until 1968, it was not possible to know how many near-misses took place each year. Pilots were always reluctant to report a near-miss for fear of disciplinary action for their part in the incident. But in January of 1968, the FAA, the agency directly charged with aviation safety for airlines and general aviation alike, granted official immunity to every pilot reporting a near-miss. This immunity was extended for the entire year of 1968.

The results were dramatic. Prior to 1968, the average monthly number of reported near-misses was about 45. In the first month of 1968, there were 233 near-misses reported. February saw 213 reported. And March saw the number rise to 241. The total of reported near-misses for all of 1968 was 2,230. This compares to slightly over 500 reported in 1967.

It is axiomatic to state that as the number of near-miss incidents rises, so does the danger of midair collision. One of the reasons for the high near-miss incident rate is the mixture of controlled and uncontrolled aircraft sharing the airspace. The system of air traffic control operated by the FAA is not and has never been capable of insuring the separation of controlled and uncontrolled aircraft in a shared airspace. And the air traffic control system has not improved very much despite the drastic increase in aviation activity in this country in the past ten years.

The number of airline operations has increased as passenger demand has become greater. In 1968, the scheduled airlines flew 114 billion revenue passenger miles (a revenue passenger mile is one mile flown by one paying passenger). That number is expected to reach 342 billion revenue passenger miles by 1979. Also in 1968, there were 55 million landings and takeoffs at airports with FAA air traffic control towers (322 airports out of a total of over 10,000). That figure should increase to 167 million by 1979, according to FAA forecasts.

This substantial increase in passenger demand, and resulting airline supply, is best considered when it is applied to specific major metropolitan airports/and airport centers. Chicago's O'Hare Airport is the nation's busiest. But its problems with increased air traffic are not as severe as those of New York's Airports. With O'Hare, that one airport is able to control all its own airspace without concern for the traffic of other nearby major airports. Not so in New York, where Kennedy, LaGuardia, and Newark airports must share the airspace of the area. Kennedy Airport can use only about 40 percent of its surrounding airspace.

Each day, New York's three airports handle thirty-five hundred flights, with fourteen hundred of these at Kennedy alone. Less than twenty years ago, Kennedy Airport handled about eighteen thousand takeoffs and landings a year. In 1968, it handled over five hundred thousand takeoffs and landings. Twenty-two and a half million passengers came and went at Kennedy in 1968. It will soon be up to 40 million.

We're air safety a matter for only two of the three safety partners—the airlines and the government-run air traffic control system—things would be fairly stable. The air traffic control system (ATC), antique in terms of the day's needs, could manage if it had to cope with just the closely controlled airline traffic equipped with all its advanced and sophisticated control and navigation hardware. There are only approximately two thousand aircraft operated by the airlines. The introduction of the jet engine, with its virtually unending capacity for work, has allowed the airlines to make great use of each aircraft. Too, larger jet aircraft, soon to be in operation by most airlines, will enable more passengers to be transported with fewer planes (provided terminal buildings and baggage systems can withstand the crush of so many people at one time). The airlines are heavily committed to the purchase of new aircraft for the future—the total fleet should increase to about thirty-nine hundred aircraft by 1979—with the expense to the airlines for this new equipment at about $10.5 billion in the next ten years.

But enter the third partner in aviation. Enter general and private aviation, with a current fleet of approximately 130,000 aircraft, 550,000 licensed pilots, and a growth expectation that will raise those figures to over 200,000 aircraft and 850,000 pilots by 1979. Consider an increase in total flying hours for general and private aviation from 24.1 million hours in 1968 to 40.9 million hours by 1979.

All this growth for the users of the aviation system is occurring while the air traffic control system remains incapable of handling the traffic of today. *And* both the federal government and general/private aviation stand firm against any changes in the regulations that would upgrade the proficiency of pilots flying the smaller planes and impose needed controls over their operations in the system.

See-and-be-seen is not the only outmoded operating concept in the aviation system. Another is an equally time-honored system known as "first come, first served." Under this anachronism, an air traffic controller is required, by regulation, to accept and treat all aircraft equally as they enter his control zone. He must do this despite the fact that two hundred passengers in a commercial jet may be inconvenienced while a single-engine private plane containing one pleasure-flying pilot slowly plods through the landing pattern ahead of the jet. His presence might even force the pilot of the airline jet to slow down to maintain adequate separation between the aircraft. The fatal crash of a Scandinavian Airlines DC-8 on January 13, 1969, into the ocean eight miles from Los Angeles International Airport could have been caused by just such a speed correction. Although the official report on that accident, in which fifteen persons were killed, has not been released as yet by the NTSB, it was said that the pilot of the DC-8 was in conversation with the Los Angeles Control Tower and had requested information on how much he should slow down to maintain distance between himself and a private plane landing ahead of him. A reduction in power at that critical moment of landing could have caused the huge jet to crash short of its runway mark.

The increasing danger in the airspace above this nation is, unfortunately, the subject of *debate*. Only the airlines have openly acknowledged that problems do exist and have taken steps to correct the problems, at least in those areas of responsibility over which they have some control. It was the airline industry itself that decided to operate most of its flights under instrument flight rules (IFR), regardless of weather. This was done for safety reasons, the thinking behind the move predicated on the logic that pilots of fast passenger-carrying aircraft sharing common airspace should not and could not provide adequate safety from midair collision simply by looking out the window. Now, this very procedure in the interest of safety has led to debate over whether the airlines overburden the traffic control system by operating under control at all times.

Another example of airline willingness to restrict itself for safety concerns drinking and flying, a major danger area in flying today. All airlines impose their own rules, which prohibit any crew member from drinking twenty-four hours before operating a flight. There is no such rule on the books of the FAA.

One area of great debate concerns the use of near-miss statistics as a basis for evaluating the air safety picture. The entire question of near-misses has bogged down in semantics and definitions. The primary foes of using near-miss reports as indicative material have been the spokesmen for general and private aviation. Their stand is easily understood. Since virtually all airline flights are controlled on a continuous basis, regardless of weather, any changes in the air traffic system based upon near-miss findings would necessarily restrict uncontrolled flights of general and private aviation aircraft. This is but one area in which general and private aviation, through its trade associations, has brought pressure to bear. And, as in other areas of aviation debate, it has managed to prevail, enough so that needed changes have been shelved, perhaps never to be introduced again.

Of course, when a near-miss becomes a midair collision, the statistics become more meaningful and less debatable. Between 1956 and 1967, there were 206 midair collisions in which 682 persons died. Of these, 3 involved commercial aircraft; 174 involved general and private aviation aircraft, with the remainder attributed to military operations.

David D. Thomas, the deputy administrator of the FAA at the time of the Urbana midair collision, testified before hearings held following the accident by the House Committee on Interstate and Foreign Commerce and the Subcommittee on Transportation and Aeronautics. He said, "Since the traffic is growing rapidly, the potential for near-misses would be increasing." What he didn't say, but what is clearly understood, is that as near-misses increase, so does the potential for fatal midair collisions.

Those hearings at which Thomas and many others testified were not an outgrowth of Urbana alone. On the heels of the Urbana midair had come another fatal midair collision between a commercial airliner and a private plane. This accident occurred on July 19, 1967, over Hendersonville, North Carolina. Involved was a Piedmont Airlines Boeing 727, a short- and medium-haul tri-jet used by most of the major airlines, and a twin-engine Cessna 310. In this accident, the pilot of the private plane was found to have been at fault, although the NTSB also criticized the air traffic control system procedures under which the aircraft were operating. The Hendersonville midair is discussed more fully later in the book, but for now it is sufficient to understand that it was the combination of the two midair accidents in the same year, with a loss of ninety-five passenger lives, that spurred a lethargic Congress to take another look at the nation's air safety needs and problems. The fact that Navy Secretary-designate John McNaughton lost his life in the Hendersonville midair also served to hasten congressional interest. His death brought things a little closer to home.

The congressional hearings on aviation safety following Urbana were held on July 24 and August 28 and 29, 1967, with an extension of them resumed on March 26 and 27, 1968. It was the intention of the committee members to delve into all aspects of aviation safety. But it became evident early in the proceedings that the Urbana and Hendersonville tragedies would set the tone for the questioning and testimony. Near-misses and the growing danger of mixing commercial jet airliners with small, privately operated planes took center stage.

The hearings covered little new ground. They served primarily to reaffirm the *systems* concept of aviation safety and to touch upon, often with too gentle a touch, the weak links in the safety chain. The committee members leveled some criticism at the general and private aviation communities for their dogmatic resistance to change. And the FAA shared in this criticism for not recognizing and acting upon the problem areas. But for the most part, the hearings rushed along, stopping only long enough to bring a problem to light, not long enough to seek solutions. The two phrases used most often by witnesses from the FAA were "we're thinking about that" and "we're working on that." Such answers prompted Congressman Richard Ottinger of New York to say, "I am not as sanguine as some of my colleagues about the way the agency [FAA] has exercised its responsibilities in the area of air safety. I really think you have been derelict in your duty in terms of actively pursuing the reasonable things that might be done to improve air safety. . . . Your answer is always, 'We are studying it; we are looking into it. Maybe we will do something in the far future.' In view of the real crisis we are confronting, it would require action now. I think you have been derelict in your duties in not pursuing these matters more diligently."

Some of the testimony should have been of concern to anyone planning an airline trip in the future. The extent of congestion in the skies was revealed time after time by witnesses before the committees. One witness told of a specific day, February 4, 1968, at Port Columbus, the airport in Columbus, Ohio. At one time during that day, ninety-three individual targets were visible on the radar screens in the air traffic control room. All these ninety-three targets were within twenty-five miles of the airport. An American Airlines jet took off and proceeded northwest. The air traffic controller was forced to call the captain of the jet sixteen times before the airliner had climbed five thousand feet into the air. The American captain was able to identify about twelve of the aircraft reported to him by the controller as being in his airspace.

And of the total ninety-three targets on the radar screen made by aircraft in the control zone, the controller knew the altitude of only 10 percent. This 10 percent comprised those aircraft that either had reported their altitude to the controller by radio or had filed instrument flight plans. The rest of the aircraft in the area were simply flying through the control zone at altitudes unknown to the controller, the man responsible for keeping aircraft apart.

Such testimony indicates two obvious failings in the system: aircraft are free to fly unrestricted through dense control zones, and our current radar equipment is not capable of determining the altitude of aircraft it is tracking. The former failing is easily corrected by a change in the FAA regulations. Industry pressure from general and private aviation has kept this from happening. In the case of the latter failing— the need for three-dimensional radar that will give altitude readings—the FAA has simply been unable to mount appropriate research and development to bring such radar into the system. These are but two areas into which this book inquires. There are many others.

This one example of a portion of one day at Columbus, Ohio, can be magnified many times when applied to such large metropolitan areas as New York, Chicago, Washington, D. C., and Los Angeles. Columbus is ranked as only a medium active airport. There are nineteen airports ranked as busier airports by the FAA.

Some other problem areas in our aviation system today include the following:

☐ There is no FAA regulation prohibiting pilots from drinking before flying.

☐ There are currently 285 airports served by scheduled airlines in the nation that do not have control towers. There are 418 airports without radar.

☐ Once a private pilot has received his license, he is never required to upgrade his proficiency, is never retested, never questioned, and never expected to keep pace with the changes in the aviation system.

☐ The medical exam for a private pilot is less difficult than that given interstate bus drivers.

☐ The FAA has turned over responsibility for testing applicants for a private pilot's license to thousands of instructors, in most cases the same instructors teaching the student pilots. The students are judged by their own, highly paid teachers. A similar situation exists with aircraft maintenance. The mechanic fixing a private plane is authorized to pass on his own work.

☐ The number of accidents in general and private aviation is now over six thousand each year.

☐ The FAA has admitted it can no longer keep track of general and private aviation because of the great growth of the industry. Yet, bound by the Federal Aviation Act of 1958 which directs the FAA to foster and promote aviation, this government agency constantly encourages more and more people to learn to fly. The manufacturers of small planes also mount impressive campaigns to encourage more people to become pilots.

☐ A private pilot needs nothing more than thirty-five hours and a radio to fly into the nation's busiest airports. He must be accepted on a first-come, first-served basis, regardless of commercial aircraft with thousands of passengers waiting for access to the airport.

☐ In 1967, commercial air carriers were delayed 130,000 hours. The time lost to the passengers on these flights amounted to 7 million man-hours. The airline industry estimates its passengers lost $300 million worth of precious time in 1968. Much of this delay was due to private airplanes using major airports.

☐ The lobby of private aviation's interests is one of the most powerful in Washington. Through its efforts, proposal after proposal offered by the FAA in the interest of improved safety has been battered down and defeated.

☐ Private pilot proficiency grows lower as the demands of aviation increase. Eighty percent of private aviation accidents are caused by pilot error or lack of judgment.

☐ In 1967, the FAA was called on to aid 3,697 pilots. Of these, 2,219 were lost. The potential danger to a commercial airliner from a lost private pilot is great.

☐ One air traffic controller recently commented to his physician, "I absolutely refuse to fly anymore. I know the mess up there." That mess is congestion and threat of midair collision.

☐ A student pilot taking the FAA written test must receive a grade of only 70 to pass. Most state driver's license written exams require a higher passing score. The 30 percent of the questions missed on the FAA exam could include those on navigation, procedures in congested airspace—anything.

☐ 30 percent of fatal general and private aviation accidents involved pilots whose blood alcohol level was above that which would impair judgment and coordination.

☐ The nation's millions of airline passengers provide the great bulk of funds to support airport development and improvements to the air traffic control system. Yet, they have the least to say about aviation matters.

☐ Airlines pay, through the 5 percent passenger excise tax, about 44 percent of the cost of the federal air traffic control system. They take up about 44 percent of its use. General and private aviation pay about 4 percent, although they use the system about 28 percent of the time.

☐ There is no central agency in which all aviation problems can be handled on an integrated basis. The FAA is responsible for safety, the CAB is responsible for the airlines as an industry, and each local community is responsible for airport planning.

Some of these problem areas were brought out during the aviation safety hearings following Urbana. But, oddly enough, the flying public didn't respond to the danger signals. It wasn't until the massive delays of the summer of 1968 that airline passengers began to complain. Evidently, inconvenience was more difficult to swallow than a threat to their safety.

That segment of aviation known as general and private aviation constitutes a definite threat to aviation safety. It is in this threatening position because of its unwillingness to accept control and modifications of the procedures necessary to insure air safety to the greatest numbers—the paying airline passengers. It has been aided in its stand and resulting position by the federal government, the body of experts charged with promoting safety in the air. The threat caused by general and private aviation is the most easily corrected of all the threats to safe air transportation. Yet little is done.

It is the intention of this book to examine general and private aviation, its stands, demands, and posture in today's aviation environment. To understand these things, it is first necessary to understand the medium in which general and private aviation performs.

CHAPTER TWO

Aviation—Public and Private

A substantial stumbling block to clear understanding of today's aviation environment is caused by difficulties in semantics and definition. The federal government and industry groups have established a set of definitions that have become widely accepted in the trade and with the general public. This chapter explains these group definitions.

However, a new set of terms and definitions must be applied to provide a more accurate picture of aviation, especially in light of the controversy between the commercial airlines and what is commonly referred to as general aviation. Therefore, in an attempt to clarify what is a complex picture, I have chosen to break aviation down into only two basic categories—*public* and *private*. Public air transportation is that serving the millions of paying passengers who share equally in the success or failure of the nation's public air transport system. Private aviation is so named in this book to denote all other civil aviation activity that, by the nature of individual and privileged participation by its users, cannot be truly defined as being for the public good and in the public interest. Were conditions such that both the public and private segments could be accommodated equally and without restriction, then there would be no need to delineate their functions. But such ideal conditions do not exist.

Consequently, for the purpose of this book the following definitions apply:

Private aviation includes all aviation activity commonly classified under the general aviation category.

Public aviation includes the activities of the commercial airlines or common carriers, as they are sometimes referred to.

Pleasure flying will denote the "flying for fun" category that is known as private aviation under the general aviation category in the prevailing "official" breakdowns. A glossary of aviation terms will be found on page 199.

The following material represents aviation as defined under prevailing. thinking. It is presented without consideration for the author's new definitions so the reader will know what has gone before.

The commercial airlines and general aviation have always made up what has been termed civil aviation. Under existing official definition, general aviation includes all aviation activity except commercial airlines and military aviation.

Civil aviation is relatively new. It began in 1903 with the Wright brothers' successful flight and has grown to its present staggering proportions. This growth, and the parallel growth of the nation it serves, is at the heart of the conflict now existing between the commercial airlines and general aviation.

Early attempts at flying date back to November 1783, when Jean François Pilâtre de Rozier and the Marquis François Laurent d'Arlandes made the first man-carrying free balloon flight.

A natural progression of experiments led to the airships of the latter part of the nineteenth century—the dirigibles. From there, man worked with the notion of steam-powered aircraft. Many attempts using steam as the power source were attempted, but none succeeded.

Man-carrying gliders were also part of the experimental

aviation progression, and were actually the prime source of inspiration for the Wright brothers.

Throughout all the years of early aviation, a marked spirit of recklessness and glamour permeated the minds and hearts of its participants and spectators. Here was man entering an unnatural state, willingly facing death, grappling with nature. The poetry and philosophy of the day reflected the image of man in the sky. John Gillespie Magee, Jr., wrote in his sonnet, "High Flight":

> Oh! I have slipped the surly bonds of Earth
> And danced the skies on laughter-silvered wings;
> Sunward I've climbed, and joined the tumbling mirth
> Of sun-split clouds. . . .

The Wright brothers' successful flight in 1903 brought aviation to America. In 1908, Glenn Curtiss's *Junebug* made the first public flight of over a kilometer in the United States. Competition for distance and speed brought a continuous stream of new records to the infant industry. And while the average citizen looked upon aviators with some awe, most were convinced that flying was nothing more than a device for daredevils. Needless to say, those engaged in flying in those early days were pleased with the image. The aviator was the outstanding athlete, wire walker, fire-eater, and soldier rolled into one. A great deal of this hero image is still found in many private pilots.

Aviation remained general aviation until 1926, when the first regularly scheduled air service was founded that offered any real promise of the future. In effect, this constituted the introduction of civil aviation's second segment—the commercial airline.

Passengers had little to do with this step into commercial aviation. It was the United States mail, now allowed to be carried by private operators under the Kelly Act of 1925, that enticed the early pioneers into the business of aviation.

The mail continued as the primary revenue for the airlines until President Franklin Roosevelt ordered cancellation of air-mail contracts with private operators, and in 1934 ordered the Army Air Corps to carry the mail. The airlines were left with airplanes and pilots, but nothing to transport.

Why not people? There had been some daring citizens who'd flown as passengers on the early mail flights. In fact, 5,782 passengers had flown with the airlines in 1926. And the number had increased each year between 1926 and 1934. Perhaps enough people could now be lured into the sky as paying passengers to support the airlines.

That decision proved pure inspiration. In 1934, the nation's airlines carried 461,743 passengers. The figure rose to 4,060,545 by 1942. And 1968's 150 million passengers further justified the faith of 1934.

As the airlines grew, so did their partner in civil aviation, general aviation. In 1956, the manufacturers of general aviation aircraft delivered $81.1 million worth of these aircraft (the nature of general aviation aircraft is explained on page 29). By 1966, that figure stood at $492.5 million. These figures reflect domestic deliveries only. Since 1962, the manufacturers have been delivering on the average of 854 new general aviation aircraft each month. There are currently about 130,000 general aviation aircraft in the United States. By 1979, the number is expected to rise to over 200,000.

In 1966, general aviation aircraft were flown 21,023,000 hours. In 1967, they were flown 22,200,000 hours. The Federal Aviation Administration estimates they will fly 40.9 million hours by 1979.

As more and more airplanes took to the air, and more citizens turned to the airlines for public transportation, a moral and practical need arose for government control. It became evident there would have to be stop signs in the sky, rights-of-way, warning lights, and traffic policemen to insure an orderly and safe flow of air traffic. The young airline industry was in favor of an orderly system of control. General aviation was not. It viewed such controls as threats to its growth and freedom.

The federal government had anticipated the potentials of civil aviation as far back as 1915. It established in that year a National Advisory Committee for Aeronautics (NACA) to "supervise and direct the scientific study of the problems of flight, with a view to their practical solution." This committee sought to have legislation passed for the orderly development of civil aviation. President Woodrow Wilson submitted a bill to Congress in 1919 that had been drafted by NACA. The bill would have authorized the Department of Commerce to license pilots, inspect machines, and supervise the use of airfields. This proposed legislation was defeated.

Other aviation bills were introduced every year after that, but it wasn't until 1926 that any meaningful legislation came on the books, in this case the Air Commerce Act. This act was described by its drafters as "the legislative cornerstone for the development of commercial aviation in America." It also created the *system* in which civil aviation would live and operate.

The system was initially large enough to accommodate its users—the airlines and general aviation. But as each swelled in size and demand, the system began falling behind in its capability to control the users. It never caught up. Today, the nation's scheduled airlines stand in confrontation with general aviation. The system is about to burst, the skies are no longer big enough for both.

For the airline passenger of 1969 and beyond, such dialogue of confrontation is irrelevant. The airline passenger wishes only to fly safely, and on time, from one point to another. He demands, and should receive, assurances that intra-industry battles, government bureaucratic incapabilities, and self-serving special interest group pressures will not hinder his goal of safe and efficient travel. It is the paying airline passenger who suffers the most when aviation's ills are compounded by such factors.

There is a crisis in aviation today. This is not an overstatement of the fact. Nor is it excessively strong to state that a battle is being waged at the passenger's expense. The cost to him may be in lost time. Or it may cost him his life.

On one side of the aviation arena stand the scheduled airlines. On the other side, general aviation. And officiating the bout is the federal government, an ironic situation since the federal government started the battle in the first place. Were a program written and printed for the spectators to the battle, in this case the airline passengers of America, it would necessarily contain the following information.

THE AIRLINES

There are three classifications within the airline category of civil aviation. Of these, one is most significant to the majority of airline passengers. This is the category known as *certified route air carriers*. There are forty-nine airlines within this category, each serving cities within the United States on a regularly scheduled basis. Some are known as trunk lines. These are the largest airlines, and serve cities across the nation. The others are known as regional carriers, and serve cities within set geographical boundaries. Together, the trunk and regional carriers serve the large majority of air passengers. The trunk carriers include such familiar names as Eastern, American, Trans World (TWA), United, Braniff, Delta, Northeast, Northwest, and Western. The regional carriers include Allegheny, Bonanza, Central, Frontier, Lake Central, Mohawk, Ozark, Pacific, Piedmont, Trans Texas, and West Coast. Also included in the certified route air carrier category are intra-Alaskan and intra-Hawaiian airlines, international and territorial passenger airlines such as Pan American and Air America, and all-cargo airlines including Airlift International, Flying Tiger, and Slick.

The fleets of aircraft utilized by these carriers are changing in their type and performance capabilities. Each year sees more and more piston (propeller-driven) aircraft phased out in favor of jet aircraft. A little over 60 percent of aircraft now in service with the airlines are jet powered. There are now approximately three hundred piston aircraft left in the airline fleet. The FAA forecasts this number will drop to about two hundred in 1970. And the early seventies should see all airlines using all-turbine aircraft.

The remaining two types of operations listed under the airline category of civil aviation are the *supplemental air carriers* and *commercial operators*. The supplemental air carriers are those that do not fly specified routes on a regularly scheduled basis, but fly as charter aircraft for groups and tours.

The commercial operations also fly without regular schedules or routes. They are smaller than the supplemental airlines and utilize smaller aircraft, which are hired out to smaller groups of people.

But, as mentioned earlier, it is the certified route air carriers that are most significant in the current aviation crisis. For the purpose of identification, the use of the term *airline* in this book will refer to these air carriers, unless noted otherwise.

The nation's airlines operate a fleet of aircraft numbering about 2,500. This is expected to rise to almost 4,000 by 1979, according to FAA figures. In 1968 the airlines took delivery of 451 new planes at a total cost to them of $2.6 billion. Their commitments for new aircraft total $7.6 billion by 1971.

The airlines currently employ more than 250,000 people with a total payroll expenditure of over two billion dollars a year.

GENERAL AVIATION

General aviation includes all civil aviation except the airlines. Included in the catchall phrase general aviation are the following:

Business Aviation.   There are currently about nineteen thousand business firms that own, or lease, and operate aircraft for business use. These firms account for about twenty-three thousand general aviation aircraft, which range from single-engine planes to highly sophisticated, pure jet aircraft. They range from such corporate giants as General Motors, Mobil Oil, U. S. Steel, and B. F. Goodrich to the smallest companies with only a few employees. The larger firms naturally have larger fleets of aircraft, which usually include more advanced types of equipment. It is also usual for the larger firms to employ professional pilots and to operate their fleets of planes from flight offices within the company. These flight offices in larger firms function much as the airlines do, including the use of route-planning facilities, dispatch offices, and scheduling personnel.

The smaller firms may or may not employ professional pilots. In many cases, company personnel who have taken flying lessons operate the company aircraft for business trips.

According to a survey by *Aviation Week and Space Technology* in 1962, eighty-five of the top hundred companies in America owned and operated their own aircraft.

Business aviation is a two-billion-dollar-a-year business, according to the National Business Aircraft Association (NBAA), the trade association representing corporate flying interests.

Private Aviation.   This group makes up the largest single group within general aviation. It consists of individuals who fly for fun. These individuals generally operate the smaller single-engine aircraft, which are the least expensive to purchase or rent and to operate.

Most pilots in this classification hold a private pilot certificate, the basic license which permits qualified persons to fly. A private pilot may take passengers, but not charge them. He may receive his license after a minimum of thirty-five hours of instruction. In 1968, the most recent year for which figures are available, there were 281,728 pilots with the basic private license.

Instructional Aviation. It is in this area of general aviation that pilots are trained. In 1968, there were 209,406 student pilots. This is an increase of over 28,000 student pilots from 1967.

Industrial Aviation. This category includes such aviation activity as fire fighting, crop-dusting, pipeline inspection, ambulance service, police and rescue work, survey and geological exploration, traffic reporting, and other related industrial missions. It constitutes a small percentage of general aviation.

Air Taxi. The air taxi industry consists of thousands of small aircraft and pilots that link suburban and rural areas with larger towns and cities. Many air taxis fly airline passengers into major airports from outlying suburban airports.

The most recent figures, for 1966, show there were 3,017 air taxi operators flying 11,063 aircraft on a part-time or full-time basis. Air taxis carried 4.7 million passengers in 1966, flew almost 3 million hours, and accounted for 13 percent of all general aviation activity.

Although categorized as general aviation, the FAA has pressed to bring the air taxi industry into the airline classification. The shift in classification involves a recent government awareness of the air taxi role in public transportation. As an example, 1966's figures, which showed 4.7 million citizens utilizing air taxis for transportation, have caused the National Transportation Safety Board (NTSB) and the FAA to reconsider allowing air taxis to operate with minimal control. General aviation's accident record has been worsening, with air taxis leading the way. (The air taxi industry is covered more fully in a subsequent chapter.)

General aviation boasts 98 percent of all civil aircraft, with 34 percent of general aviation aircraft consisting of single-engine, propeller-driven planes. At the end of 1968, there were more than 130,000 general aviation aircraft.

To many people, general aviation is synonymous with the Piper Cub, that tiny single-engine aircraft of the thirties in which thousands of pilots learned to fly. You can still buy a Piper Cub for about two thousand dollars, and there are numerous flight schools in the United States at which the Piper Cub J-3 is the basic training aircraft for student pilots. But it is as erroneous to use the Piper Cub as a symbol of general aviation today as it would be to use the Model T Ford as an automotive symbol. The aircraft now in use by general aviation pilots span the entire range of aircraft development and production. There are currently over ten models of twin-engine, pure jet aircraft in the general aviation fleet, ranging in price from $595,000 to $2.5 million. These jets cruise in the range of five hundred miles per hour and possess navigation equipment found on the most sophisticated airline jet planes. These jets are, of course, a small percentage of general aviation's fleet, but are indicative of the growing sophistication of the industry.

Over 50 percent of general aviation aircraft consist of single engine, propeller-driven planes with a seating capacity of four or more persons. This category includes a range of prices, starting with the Aero Commander at about $8,500 and going up to such aircraft as the Mooney Mustang, which sells for over $46,000. The addition of navigation equipment and radio gear beyond what is basically supplied with new aircraft can add thousands of dollars to the purchase price. There is also a variance in price between fixed-gear aircraft (the landing gear remains extended below the aircraft during flight) and retractable landing gear aircraft (the landing gear retracts into the plane's fuselage during flight). Retractable landing gear aircraft are usually faster because of the decreased drag of the airflow over the landing gear. Fixed-gear aircraft range in maximum cruising speed from 112 to 185 miles per hour. Retractable landing gear planes have cruising speeds of from 172 to 230 miles per hour.

There are a number of twin-engine, propeller-driven aircraft ranging in price from $37,000 to $250,000, and in cruising speed from 194 to 250 miles per hour.

There is also the twin-engine, turboprop category of general aviation aircraft (propellers driven by jet power), which range in price from $310,000 to over $420,000, and in cruising speed from 250 to 310 miles per hour.

Other classes include helicopters and STOL aircraft (short takeoff and landing aircraft), which are specially designed, propeller-driven airplanes capable of landing and taking off on extremely short runways. Finally, there are the gliders, balloons, and blimps.

The following table shows the types of general aviation aircraft in use and their relative proportion of the total fleet.

Single-engine (seat 1–3 persons)	32.9%
Single-engine (seat 4 or more)	52.1
Multi-engine (propeller)	12.0
Turbine (includes jet)	.6
Helicopters	1.6
Gliders, blimps, balloons	.8

It should be noted that the type of aircraft is no longer a true measure of the difference between general aviation and airline operations. A well-known publisher recently purchased for his personal use a DC-9, a twin-engine passenger jet similar to those used by many airlines. Smaller airlines are increasingly going into aircraft purchases of the type usually associated with general aviation. This crossover reinforces the need to distinguish between the airlines and general aviation on the basis of *mission*. The mission of the airlines is to transport the mass public. All other uses of aircraft fall into the category of general aviation.

There is a very large market in used GA aircraft. Certain models are in such demand that their value stands up, with almost no depreciation loss. The high cost of new airplanes prohibits many new and student pilots from purchasing them early in their flying years. They turn to used aircraft, which can be purchased for as little as fifteen hundred dollars in respectable flying condition.

Private pilots with high mechanical ability, can build their own planes. There are currently more than two thousand home-built airplanes flying in the United States. Most of these are constructed from kits and/or plans offered by various companies in the field. These aircraft range from extremely well-engineered and well-constructed equipment to slipshod, inadequate planes. The FAA is responsible for the certification of all aircraft in the United States, including home-builts.

A private pilot certificate is granted anyone over seventeen years of age who has received a minimum of forty hours of instruction (thirty-five hours from certain FAA-designated flight schools), of which at least twenty hours were solo and ten hours were solo cross-country flying. An applicant for a student pilot's certificate, the certificate used during the training phase, must be at least sixteen years old. He must also have been examined by an FAA-designated doctor within twenty-four months prior to the issuance of the student license.

Following his training, and upon reaching his seventeenth birthday, the student pilot is tested by an FAA flight examiner (more recently, an FAA-designated flight instructor, probably the same one who taught the student how to fly) on his flying skills, and is given a written test on which he must answer 70 percent of the questions correctly. Upon the successful completion of these requirements, the applicant is issued his private certificate, which enables him to fly anywhere, to carry passengers, although not for hire, and to engage in flying activity in the type of aircraft for which he has been certified. If he trained in a single-engine plane with wheels (as opposed to a seaplane), he will be licensed to operate an aircraft of that nature, although it need not be the same model or make.

After receiving his private certificate, the new pilot need never again train or be subject to retesting. Any further exposure to training is left to the discretion and desires of the flyer.

There are more than 550,000 licensed pilots in the United States, with only 25,000 of them employed by the airlines. Of the remaining 525,000, the majority hold the basic private pilot certificate (281,728 in 1968).

THE GOVERNMENT

Since passage of the Air Commerce Act of 1926, the federal government has taken an active role in aviation affairs. The Department of Commerce was originally charged with this responsibility under the act, and held this responsibility until 1938, when the Civil Aeronautics Act was signed into law by President Roosevelt. This act created a new kind of federal agency for aviation. It was called the Civil Aeronautics Authority, and consisted of a five-man board headed by an administrator appointed by the president.

The CAA reigned as the agency responsible for aviation safety until the Federal Aviation Administration (FAA) was established in 1958. The FAA is still responsible for aviation safety and for the air traffic system in which all civil aviation operates.

Today's FAA is part of the Department of Transportation (DOT), which was formed in 1966 to coordinate all national travel needs. The FAA's primary mission is to foster the development and safety of American aviation. It is responsible for the licensing of all pilots, the certification of all aircraft as airworthy, the operation of the air traffic control system in the interest of effective utilization of the airspace and to insure adequate separation of aircraft, the operation of the National Airspace System, the administration of the Federal Aid to Airports Program, and all other policy, administrative, and operational functions necessary to accomplish its mission.

The FAA employs over forty thousand people. Its headquarters is in Washington, D.C., and it operates regional offices throughout the country. Its appropriation for fiscal year 1967 amounted to $993.2 million, which was a rise of 15 percent over its budget for 1966. Its appropriation for fiscal year 1968 was down to $915 million.

The Civil Aeronautics Board (CAB), consisting of members appointed by the president, is responsible for rates and routes of the airlines in domestic operations. It plays a negligible role in aviation safety.

The National Transportation Safety Board (NTSB) was created by the same 1966 act that created the Department of Transportation. It is an autonomous agency, completely independent of the DOT. It reports directly to Congress.

NTSB was described by President Lyndon Johnson as a board "whose sole function will be the safety of our travelers." It has also been referred to as the "Supeme Court of transportation safety."

The NTSB functions as an investigatory agency for all accidents involving transportation, and is expected to make recommendations to the appropriate agencies from which improved safety might be expected.

The NTSB asked, during the hearings leading up to its formation, that it not be given any regulatory powers. Rather it felt that, by making its safety recommendations public, the weight of the public's reaction would be sufficient to insure adoption of the recommendations. The board is headed by five men appointed by the president.

THE SYSTEM

The air traffic control system (ATC) is, despite the complexity of its hardware, a simple one in conceptual terms. It is nothing more than a planned system of traffic control for airplanes, just as an automobile traffic control system regulates the flow of cars.

Obviously, the problems of control over aircraft are more difficult than for automobiles. Airplanes operate in a three-dimensional medium. Their control must include the third dimension of altitude.

Then, too, airplanes operate at speeds far greater than those of ground vehicles. And there is the further problem of an absence of easily seen and recognized landmarks from which pilots may take their bearings and cues.

The most important individual in the nation's ATC system is the *air traffic controller*. Employed by the FAA, the controllers act as traffic policemen for aircraft in the areas in which they work. Using radar and voice communication via radio, the controllers maintain separation between aircraft in their control zones by directing the path of flight, altitude, and speed of each plane as it shares the common airspace.

There are two basic areas in which control is needed. One is in areas surrounding airport facilities, especially in larger cities where air traffic is heaviest. The other involves planes in flight, from departure point to destination.

The increasing number of aircraft delays at large city airports is due to the swarm of aircraft that must be controlled. The controllers in these areas function under FAA regulations which state the physical separation that must be maintained between aircraft to insure a reasonable level of safety. The controllers in these areas must coordinate both landings and takeoffs. Present radar equipment in use by the FAA does not indicate a plane's altitude. Each pilot is responsible for informing the controller of his altitude. Controllers must also deal with the mixture of controlled and uncontrolled aircraft using the same airport. This is especially difficult, as evidenced by the Urbana, Ohio, accident.

For en route control, the FAA has established "airways." These correspond to high-speed highways. They are well known to the professional pilots who follow them between cities. These airways are controlled continuously by en route control centers. Aircraft are prohibited from crossing or following these airways without prior approval of the ground controllers, and only after filing an instrument flight plan.

THE SPOKESMEN

The combatants in the current aviation fray do little fighting for themselves. Substituted are trade associations representing each faction's interests. For example:

1. General aviation. Its primary spokesman has always been the Aircraft Owners and Pilots Association (AOPA). This association speaks for the private or pleasure pilot and is one of the two most powerful and important aviation trade associations in Washington. It boasts about 150,000 members, conducts persuasive lobbying campaigns with Congress and the FAA, and publishes a widely read membership magazine, *The AOPA Pilot.*

Corporate flying interests are represented by the National Business Aircraft Association (NBAA). Its membership consists of corporations owning and operating aircraft for their business use. Ninety-five of America's top hundred corporations belong to NBAA.

The manufacturers of general aviation aircraft belong to the Utility Airplane Council, a division of the Aerospace Industries Association.

There are numerous other groups within general aviation, each speaking for a more narrowly defined special interest. Some of these are the Lawyer-Pilots Bar Association, International Flying Farmers, National Air Taxi Conference, Association of Commuter Airlines, National Aviation Trades Association, Astro Flying Club, Aviation Distribution Manufacturing Association, Chicago Land Business Pilots Association, and the Experimental Aircraft Association.

2. The airlines. The prime spokesman for the nation's scheduled airlines is the Air Transport Association (ATA).

This trade group rivals AOPA in power and influence in Washington.

3. The controllers. Until recently air traffic controllers had no effective voice in aviation, except for various union groups that proved ineffectual when pitted against the controllers' employer, the federal government. In 1968, however, the Professional Air Traffic Controllers Organization (PATCO) was formed. The group's counsel and spokesman is F. Lee Bailey, noted trial lawyer and avid private pilot. PATCO has proved to be an effective bargaining agent for its member controllers.

The preceding definitions reflect aviation as officially defined by the federal government and the industry itself.

But, again, the reader is asked to keep in mind the author's new set of terms that separate aviation into two main categories—*public* and *private*. This more basic separation of function will be used for the remainder of the book.

CHAPTER THREE

In Defense of Mediocrity

The increasing fatalities point up a great need to examine the preparation and training of pilots in the first place and to keep them informed with respect to the potential hazards. A dangerous pilot is dangerous to us all.

Edward Slattery
National Transportation Safety Board

I decided, in the early fall of 1968, to conduct a private experiment. It was simple enough. I would go to a local airport and rent an airplane for a few hours. I chose a day of good weather, left the house early in the morning, and drove to a small private airport in the New York metropolitan area.

I arrived at the airport, parked the car, and walked to a low prefab building housing one of the airport's aircraft rental firms. I entered and spoke to one of two men behind the counter.

"Hi. Got any 150s this morning?"

The man looked out the window toward the parking apron.

"Yup." He looked down at a sheet of paper on the counter. "Got one reserved at eleven. No problem." He placed a form in front of me. "Flying local?" he asked.

"Yes," I answered. "Thought I'd get in a couple of hours. Good day for it."

"Sure is. Supposed to hold, too. License?"

I pushed my private pilot's certificate across the counter.

"Log?" he asked, not looking up. He was referring to the logbook in which pilots record their flying time.

"I don't have it with me," I said. "I've been flying 172s the past months. It's been four or five months since I've had a 150."

"No problem," the man behind the counter replied. "Not much difference. What do you want? An hour?"

"No. Give me two. Hate to waste the weather."

"Right."

The form completed, I was given the keys to a Cessna 150 aircraft, a small single-engine airplane parked on the apron outside the building. I tried to remember the things you were supposed to do during the preflight examination of an aircraft. Only one or two basic items came to mind. The plane sat there a total stranger to me. But it made little difference. I had never intended to fly the airplane. I hadn't flown an airplane in eleven years. But I did want to prove to myself that, despite the long lapse in my flying experience, I could still rent an airplane, fly it anywhere, and let those up in the air with me take their chances. All I had to do was walk and talk with confidence, lie a little, and an airplane would be mine. I saved face by going back into the rental building and telling the man behind the counter I'd forgotten a very important meeting. I thanked him and assured him I'd be back the following day. He grunted and tore up my form.

I didn't conduct this experiment as criticism of the man who rented me the plane, although I do question his business judgment. Rather, I wanted to show in a tangible manner that *once a pilot, always a pilot.*

A private pilot never has to renew his license. He is never retested. He is never given training to brush up on forgotten skills or to learn new skills required by aviation advances. He is a pilot for life. It would take an act of gross negligence or a major infraction of the FAA regulations for that agency to take as drastic a step as license revocation. In 1967, the FAA brought 2,116 actions against pilots, with 222 of these resulting in the revocation of licenses. Many of these revocations are being appealed to the National Transportation Safety Board (NTSB). The NTSB has historically been lenient in such appeals. The offenses leading to license revocation include such infractions as low-level buzz jobs over populated areas, flying while drunk, taking passengers when not certified for such operations, and violating any of the other FAA regulations for private pilots.

I tried my experiment twice. The second time, at a different airport, the manager of the rental agency denied me an aircraft unless I could produce my logbook or was willing to take at least one hour of flying instruction with one of his pilots. I agreed to the dual instruction. We flew for two hours, during which I accomplished twelve landings and takeoffs, a few basic flying maneuvers, and two stall-and-recovery exercises. My instructor was satisfied, and I was cleared to rent the plane, another Cessna 150. From the renting firm's point of view, I'd given them reasonable proof that I could now *fly* their aircraft without wrecking it.

Their concern stopped right there. I was free to take off and fly to other local airports—Kennedy, LaGuardia, or Newark—and compete with the air traffic at those major facilities, including large airline jets loaded with passengers. No one had checked to see if I knew how to use the single radio in the plane. No one had asked my knowledge of the traffic patterns and control zones in the area. They simply wanted to know that I was capable of taking the plane off and landing it safely.

The rental agency manager had acted out of sound business judgment; the aircraft was valuable to him. But only a sense of economic self-preservation had caused him to question my proficiency.

Recertification and pilot proficiency have long been a subject of debate in the aviation industry. Early this year rules changes were proposed by the FAA that would have required the periodic retesting of private pilots. And, as usual, private aviation's spokesmen submitted vehement opposition to the change. The Aircraft Owners and Pilots Association (AOPA), speaking for its 150,000 pleasure pilots, led the rebuttal. They prevailed. The rule change was dropped, just as it had been dropped early in 1968 when it was offered.

Congressman Richard L. Ottinger, a frequent critic of the FAA, commented on the rule change defeat of February, 1969, when he said, "This action is nothing more than abject surrender to a pressure group and is further evidence that the FAA really has no concept of where the national interest in air safety lies."

The fact that the FAA introduces recertification proposals each year is, at least, recognition that a problem does exist. The number of private aviation accidents grows each year. More important, the determination of the pilot as the cause grows at an even greater rate. In 1965, there were 5,196 general aviation accidents. Of these, 77.3 percent involved the pilot as a cause, if not the only cause of the accident. There was a rise in 1966, and in 1967 the pilot was cited in 82 percent of 6,115 private aviation accidents.

Figures for 1968 are not complete. However, it is safe to assume that the pilot and not malfunction of his plane will continue as the major cause of accidents.

The following table covers the period of 1957–1967 for private aviation accidents:

| | Accidents | | |
	Total	Fatal	# of Fatalities
1957	4,200	438	800
1958	4,584	384	717
1959	4,576	450	823
1960	4,793	419	787
1961	4,625	426	761
1962	4,840	430	857

	Total	Fatal	# of Fatalities
1963	4,690	482	893
1964	5,069	526	1,083
1965	5,196	538	1,029
1966	5,712	573	1,151
1967	6,115	576	1,228

The Aircraft Owners and Pilots Association, as an organization, dates back to May 15, 1939. Five Philadelphia businessmen organized the association. It was their belief that a need existed for a strong group to represent the "forgotten men of aviation," the pilots and owners of private aircraft. It also represented the official beginning of private aviation's persecution complex.

According to the Philadelphia founders of AOPA, the association was established to "promote, protect and represent the interests of aeronautics and the pursuit of flying; to promote the economy, safety and popularity of flight in aircraft and the use of aircraft, including the pilotage thereof."

The AOPA grew to become one of the largest, most vocal, and most effective voices in Washington, D.C., and the aviation community. Its members, each paying nineteen dollars a year in dues, now number over 150,000. Its staff of some 200 conducts an aggressive, day-to-day campaign to influence government and industry leaders to the private pilot's advantage.

Max Karant, vice-president of AOPA and its leading spokesman (editor of its magazine, *The Pilot*, world traveler and speaker, and a major force in AOPA's planning committees), told me during an interview, "We've grown up with our backs against the wall. We've got to dig in our heels now and fight. This is a matter of survival."

One with only a surface knowledge of the aviation industry would have to question such an extreme statement. The position claiming oppression of private aviation is born of frustration and fear. There is truly no need for winner to take all.

Private aviation is an important and integral part of the nation's transportation system. It will survive and continue to grow, despite any introduction of needed controls over its operations.

But AOPA does believe its back is to a wall, and *The Pilot* reflects AOPA's feeling that it must lash out from its cornered position. There is almost a frantic need to attack any proposal made by the FAA, Congress, or the airlines that would in any way "encroach on the individual rights of private pilots." It is much the same kind of hysteria found in the positions taken by the National Rifle Association. In both cases, the "rights" mentioned are those protected by legislative activity of the past and seldom reconsidered in light of the needs of today.

The FAA's attempt in 1968 to introduce rule changes that would require some sort of periodic upgrading of private pilots dealt primarily with mandatory periodic flight instruction and proficiency testing. The FAA issued an "Advanced Notice of Proposed Rule Making," a prescribed procedure under the Administrative Procedures Act, and invited industry comment from interested parties by April, 1968. All proposed rules and rule changes are initiated in this manner. Based upon the comments received, the agency decides whether to go forward and declare a "Formal Notice of Proposed Rule Making." More comments are invited at this second stage and, after they are considered by the FAA, a decision is made on the rule or rule change itself.

The advance notice was issued and the comments came. Most were opposed to the changes. The response came from private pilots spurred to action by AOPA's efforts through its magazine and direct mail. In its editorials on pilot recertification, AOPA never offered any concrete reasons why the suggested rule changes were bad. They based their case, for the most part, on the *FAA's lack of proof that airman upgrading would lower the accident rate*. This kind of contestable logic appealed to AOPA's membership. They heeded the call of their leaders and swamped the FAA, and their elected representatives to Congress, with protest mail.

AOPA also revealed its persecution complex in an article entitled "Issue of Mandatory Pilot Perfection Arises Again," which ran in the March, 1968, issue of *The Pilot*. It said:

"Constant reiteration of the claim that upwards of 80 percent of all general aviation accidents is due to pilot error has given the pilot a guilt complex."

AOPA did its best to soften any psychological damage to its members by putting accident statistics through the standard twisting mill. The organization is not to be faulted for this action. All segments of the industry twist statistics to prove their own points. The end result is a minimal reliance on all statistical evidence.

In APOA's case, it claimed that the increase in flying hours as compared to the increase in accidents actually indicated an improved safety record. Using its own figures as a base, it was quite correct in this claim. But the fact remains: Private aviation pilots are causing more accidents than ever before.

In commenting on the increase in pilot-involved accidents, the National Transportation Safety Board said, "We see a great need to examine the preparation and training of pilots in the first place, their certification requirements, the maintenance of their skill, and their being informed with respect to the potential hazards of general aviation flying." The NTSB's comments were reasonable in light of the statistics. But, like the FAA, the NTSB does not always act as it speaks.

Under the organization of the NTSB, it is powerless to enforce its recommendations. But in terms of the private pilot question, our concern is not whether its recommendations are adopted. Rather, the concern is whether NTSB, in the face of statistical evidence and its own statements about a need for reevaluation of private pilot training, has made any move to suggest an upgrading of private pilots.

It has not.

I personally went through the files of NTSB recommendations. During the period from March 30, 1967, through July
31, 1968, the NTSB made a total of thirty-seven recommendations to the FAA concerning aviation safety. Not one of them
dealt with the proficiency of the private pilot. Thirty-six were
recommendations directed at aircraft manufacturers. The other
recommendation was that the FAA install red warning lights on
airport taxiways that would light up in bad weather. They
based this recommendation on the accident findings of 1966,
which showed 306 general aviation accidents resulting from
pilots who hadn't bothered to check the weather prior to
takeoff. Some suggested that a regulation be passed requiring
all pilots to check weather before departing on a flight. But
NTSB decided against this, preferring the red warning light
system, already in use in the Cape Cod area, where weather
changes are rapid and frequent. The FAA turned down NTSB's
recommendation because, its said, the Cape Cod area wasn't
typical, the red light system wasn't fail-safe, and the turning
on and off of the lights would place an undue workload on
control stations.

I asked Brad Dunbar, public information officer for NTSB,
the following:

QUESTION: I'm surprised to see how few recommendations
NTSB has made to the FAA. Only thirty-seven. Why have
there been so few?

DUNBAR: I never looked at it that way. You have to take
in the fact that we are a new organization. (*Note*: NTSB
was established in 1966. I interviewed Dunbar in November, 1968.)

QUESTION: I also noticed there has not been even one
recommendation made in the area of private pilot qualifications. Yet, 80 percent of general aviation accidents
involve pilot error or lack of judgment. Why is this?

DUNBAR: This would have to be something that was based

upon a broad and comprehensive statistical study. You just can't sit here and write down some particularly pressing problem on general aviation safety from the standpoint of pilot error. We would have to take a huge mass from our data and do a computer study of this.

QUESTION: But you've been studying private pilot proficiency and its accident influence for years, both under the CAB as well as with the FAA. You've published volume after volume of these studies and have concluded that pilots cause over five thousand private aviation accidents each year. Isn't all this data enough upon which to base some sort of recommendation?

DUNBAR: I'll have to check into that for you.

Dunbar did check for me, and once again cited the need for further study as the reason for no recommendations.

Obviously, there are many factors and requisites that go into the making of a private pilot. He must possess certain minimum physical and mental levels of competence. His training must conform to standards established by the FAA. He must pass certain written and practical tests in order to receive his license. And he must continue to meet certain criteria in order to maintain his flying privilege. But in this writer's opinion the levels prescribed by the FAA are far too low in both demand and intent.

A study by the Aircraft Development Service of the FAA in the fall of 1968 showed that 51 percent of private pilots fly less than fifty hours a year, and that only 21 percent fly more than one hundred hours a year. Forty percent of the private pilots included in the study group indicated they'd gone three months or longer during the twenty-four months preceding the study without logging any flight time.

It has been acknowledged by many people in the FAA, NTSB, and even AOPA that periodic retraining for private pilots would be a valuable course to follow. But, as with so many issues, knowing the needs, and taking concrete steps to fill those needs, are two distinct propositions.

The FAA's proposals for pilot recertification have been general in nature. In issuing the advance notice of the 1968 proposal, it said, "There is no conclusive proof as to the percentages of general aviation accidents that might have been prevented by periodic instruction, refresher training or proficiency checking. However, a review of the accident records shows that many accidents can be ascribed to deterioration of basic airmanship and skills and to pilot's failure to keep abreast of new developments and operational procedures. In this connection, much work done by the military services shows that, in particular, procedural knowledge and activities are rapidly forgotten with time and non-use."

The FAA also noted that its efforts to encourage private aviation pilots to secure periodic refresher training and proficiency checks voluntarily had been only partially successful. "Accordingly," it said, "some rulemaking action in this area may be appropriate."

The FAA's 1968 proposal for pilot recertification suggested that the holder of a private pilot certificate should be required to have a specified number of hours of flight instruction from an appropriately rated flight instructor within a fixed period (for instance, up to three hours within a six-month period or six hours within a twelve-month period) before acting as pilot of any flight that involved the carriage of persons or property. The precise maneuvers and procedures to be performed during the instruction period would not be specified by the FAA but would be left to the judgment of the flight instructor.

Such proposals for periodic instruction are, in light of existing regulations, mild and minor improvements. Regulations now on the FAA books state a private pilot must have made at least five takeoffs and five landings to a full stop within ninety days in an airplane of the same class and type before he can carry passengers. The FAA proposals

have never attempted to close the loophole ". . . before he can carry passengers with him." Alone, the private pilot can fly anywhere without as much as ten minutes' instruction, no matter how long it has been since he last piloted an aircraft. Only the business acumen of an aircraft renting company stands between a rusty pilot and an airplane. And even this breaks down too often, as evidenced by my own related experience.

Charles "C.O." Miller, director of the Bureau of Aviation Safety at NTSB, told me of an experience he had three or four years ago in California. He hadn't piloted an aircraft in ten years and was curious about what would happen if he went out to a local airport and tried to rent a plane.

"I went out one afternoon and told them I possessed a commercial license and a thousand hours of jet time but hadn't flown in a long time," Miller said. "They told me it wouldn't take very long for me to become qualified again. They said it was just like swimming; once you learn, you never forget. They gave me a fifteen or twenty minute ground briefing and up we went. We did a couple of stalls, flew in and out of the landing pattern, and came down. They never gave me any emergency training. I did nothing but simply fly the airplane. I did one more hour of this the following week and they cleared me for solo flight. By the way, I never did show them my log to back up the experience I'd spoken of. I went back one more time and told them I'd like to become nighttime-rated for flying. We went up one hour, did a few stalls, landed a few times, and I was cleared for night flying. Frankly, I think the rules in this area are pretty lousy. They're just an open invitation to bad pilot judgment and error."

Miller is in a position to make recommendations to the FAA concerning these rules. To my knowledge, he has not made any such recommendations.

Some members of the FAA feel man's sense of self-preservation will prohibit him from flying without appropriate recent training. This subject came up during a lengthy interview with Dr. Mervin K. Strickler, Jr., special assistant for aviation education for the FAA, and Ralph Lovering, special assistant to the assistant administrator for general aviation affairs.

REPORTER: Isn't the lack of any recertification program a problem in aviation safety?

LOVERING: No, I don't think so.

STRICKLER: Let me cite an example. Are you flying currently?

REPORTER: No.

STRICKLER: Why not?

REPORTER: A combination of factors. Lack of confidence in myself flying in the system. I don't know enough.

LOVERING: The sophistication of the system frightens you?

REPORTER: Yes, unless I were to go out and gain further experience and training. I don't wish to do this so I don't fly anymore.

STRICKLER: You have just stated what is probably the single most significant control in aviation.

REPORTER: What is?

STRICKLER: There is a lot of self-control for people like ourselves who keep themselves out of the system. To put it another way, people are pretty cautious about their own welfare. I don't think the people in the general public give enough credence to the strong role that the self-preservation function plays in aviation safety.

REPORTER: Except that most general aviation accidents are caused by pilot error and lack of judgment. You can't practice self-preservation unless you know your capabilities. It would seem these pilots cited in the statistics either didn't know their capabilities, or didn't care about self-preservation.

LOVERING: Most accidents are attributed to this. Not just aviation.

REPORTER: I wonder if the self-preservation sense is really as strong as it should be.

STRICKLER: No, it isn't, and I wish it were stronger.

In theory, self-preservation would prevent a lot of things. But the theory collapses when each man must be depended upon to judge accurately his own ability and plan his actions accordingly. This has not been the case in many private aviation accidents. Private pilots are notorious for overreaching their boundaries of ability, experience, and judgment. For example, on December 26, 1965, Philip T. Ippolito landed his Aeronca 7AC on the George Washington Bridge, which crosses the Hudson River between New York and New Jersey. Fortunately, the aircraft only brushed a truck, and the plane's occupants received minor injuries.

On March 2, 1967, the FAA suspended Ippolito's private pilot certificate for six months. It charged Ippolito had failed to familiarize himself with all available information concerning the flight. It charged that he had failed to secure the fuel cap on the aircraft, and did not know the suitable emergency landing sites (part of the training for student pilots), was not familiar with the operational characteristics of the aircraft, and had placed himself in a position in which a mistake in judgment would create a hazard to the life and property of others.

Ippolito appealed the FAA's decision to the National Transportation Safety Board, and it overruled the FAA. Ippolito is as free as ever to fly over and through the New York area and its stack-up of airliners. His judgment, which had led him to land his plane on a busy, major public trafficway, was upheld by the NTSB. Ippolito did, without question, have a strong sense of self-preservation.

In the October, 1967, issue of *Aerospace Medicine* was an article by Dr. Harry L. Gibbons, Judith Plechus, and Dr. Stanley R. Mohler, chief of the FAA's Aeromedical Applications Division. It dealt with six case histories in which private pilots had committed suicide while at the controls of their aircraft. In effect, these six people had used their airplanes as suicide vehicles. In some cases, a high blood alcohol level was found to have been present at the time of the suicide act.

One case involved a student pilot who, without authorization, took a plane at night, flew wingovers (rolls), stalled, and crashed. He left a note indicating his intention to take his life. He'd been discharged from the military after a mine explosion had caused moderately severe wounds of the top and side of his head. It was reported he suffered from blackout spells, although his medical examination by the FAA-authorized doctor did not indicate any of this.

Another case involved a nurse who had been operated on for breast cancer. Convinced the operation had not been successful, she put herself under psychiatric care. Her psychiatrist told her she should not fly alone. She told another doctor she planned to kill herself by crashing in the ocean. She eventually did take her life by flying her airplane into the ground. Her fears had been unfounded; the operation had been a success.

A doctor was the subject of another case history. He held a student pilot certificate and had failed his FAA written exam eight months prior to taking his life. (His test score was 44; 70 is needed to pass.) Failure of this test does not prohibit a student pilot from flying solo.

The doctor, after repeated low-level "buzz jobs" over residential areas in his hometown, finally went to his death as the aircraft crashed just outside town after stalling during one of its low-level flights.

It is estimated by Dr. Mohler and the Federal Air Surgeon of the FAA, Dr. P.V. Siegel, that about a dozen suicides occur each year in which a general aviation aircraft is the suicide vehicle. In many of these cases, the subject has a background of psychological disturbance and mental disorder. But under the medical regulations set forth by the FAA, the bulk of the doctor's knowledge comes from what the applicant tells him. As the article in *Aerospace Medicine* pointed out, aviation medical examiners occasionally work with less information than a veterinarian. A fuller discussion of the medical examination process occurs later in the book.

It is foolhardy and naïve to depend on a person's sense of self-preservation as a deterrent to his endangering others who share his airspace. Certainly the nation's 150 million airline passengers should receive a more positive assurance from the appropriate government authority that those sharing that airspace have, at least, mastered the minimums of flying proficiency, are medically able to exercise mental and physical control of their aircraft, and have expended some energy in the recent past to upgrade their skills and proficiency. As it now stands, the passenger has no such assurances.

It would take literally volumes of large catalogs to list all the general aviation accidents resulting from a basic lack of pilot judgment. The number is increased substantially when you include all the misleading "weather-induced" accidents. It is a rare occurrence in which the weather has *caused* an accident. In almost every weather-induced accident, it was the pilot's lack of knowledge, information, interest, or judgment that led him into dangerous weather conditions that already existed.

The overall lack of private pilot judgment can also be measured, in part, by the number of "saves" announced each year by the FAA. These announcements are made with a great deal of pride; the agency uses them to indicate the dedication and skill of its ground controllers who lend these assists to airmen in trouble.

Primarily, the "saves" involve private pilots who contact FAA ground control facilities and advise them of a problem, that they, the private pilots, have encountered. In most cases, the pilot is lost in or above clouds and/or bad weather. Perhaps he's in the clouds and has become disoriented without any reference to the ground or the horizon. Or he may simply be flying above the clouds, has no knowledge of instruments, and is afraid to descend through the clouds for fear of striking another airplane or, if the clouds are low enough, the ground.

The FAA celebrates its saving of these pilots. It issues glowing news releases, uses the figures in its never-ending quest for increased federal funds, and assures the private aviation community that it stands ready to assist the amateur pilot. All of this is natural enough; it is no more than practicing the basic definition of public relations—*do good and tell about it.*

But to others in the aviation industry, these "saves" do nothing more than indicate that an appalling number of private aviation pilots *don't know where they are.* They are flying under visual flight rules (VFR) in or above instrument flight rules (IFR) weather, the same weather through which the nation's airliners fly.

The number of pilots saved by the FAA each year is not small.

Year	Number of Saves
1965	2978
1966	3350
1967	3697
1968	4092

The force of self-preservation as a regulatory substitute has not proved itself. The only possible answer is a strong regulatory program dealing with improved pilot training and screening, and a system of retraining and retesting. During the House committee hearing on aviation safety in the summer of 1967, Congressman James T. Broyhill of North Carolina brought up the subject of recertification to General William F. McKee, administrator of the FAA, and to David D. Thomas, his deputy.

BROYHILL: An airline pilot receives training and retraining in the course of his career as an airline pilot. Are private pilots required to take any retraining or recertification at any time?

THOMAS: No, sir, they are not.

BROYHILL: Has the FAA ever gone into this, to see whether you should require recertification?

THOMAS: Yes, sir, we have several times in the past. As a matter of fact, we are right now. Anything we would do in this regard obviously has to be handled under rulemaking, where we go out [to the industry] for comment. We do think that reexamination by the FAA or checking out by an instructor, or some demonstrations of recent experience would be helpful.

McKEE: I think your point is well taken, Mr. Broyhill. We recognize it and are moving in this direction.

The moving has been slow. In fact, it never really started, despite the optimistic statements of Thomas and General McKee. Bound by the Administrative Procedures Act, the FAA and other regulatory agencies must solicit comments from the industries involved in their proposed rule making. In the case of the recertification proposal, private aviation, led by AOPA, has made certain the industry was heard loud and clear. The proposed rule changes were dropped each time they were introduced. In reality, the industry to be regulated in the interest of public safety has effectively controlled the very agency charged such regulation. On paper, the FAA is the body of aviation experts with the responsibility of effecting changes in regulations as needed to keep pace with aviation's growth. In fact, and despite what it says on paper, the FAA does no more than what the industry wishes. The proverbial tail wags the dog, the aircraft flies the pilot, and the private aviation industry administers its regulatory agency.

Like so many bureaucracies, the FAA cites a lack of funds

for many of its shortcomings. In some instances, there is reason for this defense. But in matters such as pilot recertification, funding plays too small a part to be listed as a reason for avoiding the issue. Westchester Congressman Richard Ottinger spoke of this during the hearings of 1967.

"You are the only technical agency in the government that is responsible for air safety," Ottinger said. "And it seems to me that your responsibility is to define the needs for improvement in air safety, whether or not you can get the Bureau of the Budget approval for them. You are the one agency of the government to which we in Congress and to which the public can look for a definition of what is reasonably needed. We look to you, as the experts, for this information. You, as the experts, should define for us what is needed and what could materially improve air safety in the United States."

Ottinger went on to list a number of areas he felt constituted a danger to air safety, including the lack of recertification program for private pilots. He also leveled a number of general charges at the FAA, most of which dealt with what he termed "negligence" on the agency's part in not pursuing air safety more aggressively. He introduced an excerpt from an article that appeared in *Electronics Magazine*. It read:

"Of all the thousands of Government agencies, it would seem almost impossible to rate one as the worst, yet technical men who have studied the air traffic control problems are ready to give that malodorous distinction to the FAA. The agency born to perform great feats of technical innovation has turned out to be weak, ineffectual, unimaginative and apathetic. The threat of midair collision hanging over the United States when the FAA was formed is still with us, only worse than ever. And the FAA is as far from coping with this threat as it was on the day it was founded."

General McKee branded the article "irresponsible."

Congressman Benjamin S. Rosenthal, whose district includes LaGuardia Airport in Queens, New York, has been the most vocal of critics of private aviation on the Hill. He recently stated, "General aviation is against restriction of any kind. It's a frontier atmosphere, as far as they're concerned, but we've left the frontier period. It's not the twenties and thirties anymore. Today, you learn to fly, or buy an airplane, and you have far more rights than you deserve."

But, like other critics of private aviation, Rosenthal also recognizes its value to the nation. He has commented, "General aviation has a role to play, but let them take their place in the sun." Just what private aviation's place should be in today's aviation medium is subject to strenuous debate. AOPA's stand has been that the individual private pilot should, in no way, be restricted in his operations. AOPA feels his training is sufficient to allow him access to all airspace. To demand any periodic retraining and recertification would place what AOPA feels is an excessive burden on the individual pilot. Section 104 of the Federal Aviation Act of 1958 guarantees freedom to all pilots in all the navigable airspace. AOPA and other industry spokesmen fall back time and again on this antiquated section of The Act.

On the other hand, critics of private aviation and its operations protest such freedom. It is their opinion that the nation and its millions of airline passengers can no longer tolerate the dangerous mix of aircraft now prevalent in the airspace. There is a growing conviction that when you mix sophisticated, high-performance aircraft, piloted by highly skilled and experienced professional pilots, with private-interest, smaller and slower aircraft piloted by inexperienced and often incapable pilots, only disaster can result. The near-miss statistics and midair accidents such as at Urbana, Ohio, and Hendersonville, North Carolina, would seem to lend some credence to the latter position.

There are, of course, many skilled and experienced private pilots. Arthur Godfrey is a dedicated pilot with thousands of flying hours. He is acknowledged by airline pilots as fully qualified and proficient. There are many others like him who take their flying seriously and continue to work at upgrading their abilities and capabilities.

But of the over five hundred thousand private pilots flying today, such skilled airmen are but a small percentage of the total.

The actual training standards of a private pilot do not vary with geographical location of the student's training. This is an important consideration when dealing with any analysis of the private pilot's qualifications. In my own case, my training was taken in Lafayette, Indiana, a college town (Purdue University) of less than 50,000 population. The airport at which my training was taken experienced minimum air traffic, most of it private interest aircraft. Lake Central Airlines, a regional airline, came into Lafayette a few times each day and then only in good weather conditions. Consequently, the flying performed by student and private pilots constituted little danger to passengers on scheduled airlines.

Too, training at Lafayette placed few demands on the student pilot to become familiar with procedures and operations in high-density air traffic hub areas. Flying under visual flight rules (VFR) was sufficient for anyone utilizing the Lafayette Airport.

The problem comes when a student pilot from an area such as Lafayette receives his private pilot certificate and moves to New York, Los Angeles, Chicago, or Washington, D.C. Or, without an actual move, the same problem occurs when the newly certified pilot decides to take a cross-country flight to one of these high-density areas. He is free to do this. He is free to fly anywhere on his Lafayette-gained license. And yet he is totally unprepared to conduct a flight through those busy air corridors where airline traffic is thick and aircraft separation is paramount to survival. The demands placed upon any pilot navigating these busy hub areas are numerous and difficult, at least if the pilot wishes to fly with assurance and to make use of all the air traffic control safeguards. But he doesn't have to use them. He needs only one working radio in his plane. And he is free to penetrate the area, an area in which numerous airline jets are in the process of preparing for landings or clearing the area after taking off, all under continuous ground control.

The private pilot from Lafayette, Indiana, is to be accepted for landing at the airport on a first-come, first-served basis. The FAA air traffic control personnel are bound by regulation to treat all aircraft equally and to handle them in order of their appearance on the scene. As a consequence, huge jets filled with paying passengers must circle needlessly while a single-engine private plane, piloted by someone as young as seventeen and possessing no more than thirty-five flying hours, lands in front of them. This is another *tradition* defended by private aviation's spokesmen. To establish priorities, they say, would discriminate against the individual. Whether the maintenance of this anachronistic concept discriminates against the millions of airline passengers who suffer from it does not seem to be a consideration.

John Carroll, chief of the Accident Prevention Branch at NTSB, and a commercially and instrument-rated pilot with thousands of hours, has rather strong feelings about the training of private pilots.

"We have a situation that alarms me," he said during an interview. "Some manufacturers and flying schools are operating at the minimum standards specified by the Federal Air Regulations [written by the FAA]. It's incumbent upon us here to determine what the gap is between those operating above the minimums and those operating just at the minimum levels. That gap has to be closed by raising the minimum standards wherever possible."

Carroll, who came to his job with NTSB after extensive periods with the FAA and CAB and as administrator of the Flight Safety Foundation's Crash Injury Investigator School, feels that pilot training has changed for the worse since his training in the forties.

"I have no basis for saying this," he noted, "but I just have this gut feeling that flight training being given new pilots today is inferior to what I received during my training. They don't even teach spins anymore. The performance characteristics of aircraft after the war started to really move up fast, and the spin characteristics became much more dangerous. The way they treated it was to placard the airplane instructing the pilot that the airplane should not be intentially spun. Once you got into a spin with it, you had a slim chance of getting out of it. This would indicate that the pilot ought to know more about spins and handling them than he ever did before. But they don't even bother to teach it today. Instructors have taken the attitude that if you weren't allowed to spin the airplane because the placard said so, there was no sense bothering to teach about spins. That's the reverse, it seems to me, of what it should have meant to the instructors."

The argument has been presented that the federal government has no business trying to protect the individual from himself. The proponents of this line of thinking feel that if a private pilot wishes to fly without upgrading himself, that's his business and he should suffer the consequences. John Carroll had some thoughts on this subject, too.

"The government does have a very distinct responsibility to the guy who doesn't know enough to take care of himself," Carroll said. "It might be less of a responsibility where the guy has only himself to consider. If he is flying out over some barren desert, the worst he can do is put a hole in the sand. But when you get into high-density areas like New York and Chicago and Washington, and you begin conflicting with airline operations, then there is probably a logic that can be applied with good moral backing that would say you have to exercise more control and better control over a situation where grandma and the kids are stepping up and buying their tickets."

The problems caused by mixing airline aircraft and private

aircraft in high-density areas are well known to anyone who flies with any regularity out of major air traffic hubs. I have sat for long periods of time in an airline jet while other departing aircraft lined up in front of us. Often, the line in front was studded with small, private aircraft. Not only do they constitute a maddening delay simply by being there, their single pilot delaying thousands of passengers, but their slow performance characteristics further delay the takeoff flow from the airport. American Airlines, the airline that has been the most direct and outspoken in the current controversy, has performed studies that indicate that 75 percent of all aircraft operations at airports served by the nation's airlines are private aviation activity. FAA studies bear out American's figures, and further forecast this percentage to rise to 85 by 1977. Of course, such a mix of airline and private aviation aircraft is especially crucial at the major traffic hubs. For instance, 43 percent of all activity at New York's LaGuardia Airport has been private aviation. Other large traffic areas have experienced similar percentages: Cleveland, 52 percent; St. Louis, 57 percent; Dallas, 39 percent; Newark, 21 percent; Boston, 32 percent; and Washington National, 27 percent. In the New York area airports, percentages diminished following an increase in the landing fees charged private planes by the Port of New York Authority, the bistate agency that operates the facilities. The fees were raised in 1968 from five dollars to twenty-five dollars per landing for private planes, a move announced with the deliberate intention to discourage private aircraft from using the larger airports. It worked, despite vehement protestations from AOPA.

John Carroll told me a story that typifies what a professional pilot operating on instrument flight rules (IFR) encounters at many large airports.

"I've spent twenty to twenty-five minutes setting up an instrument landing approach at Washington National Airport," he said, "and have been on my final approach for landing when the controller has told me to pull up and go around again because a private plane flying visual flight rules has entered the area and is a hazard to other aircraft. That means setting up my IFR all over again. It happens many times with airline pilots, too."

As evidenced by the Urbana tragedy, many private planes entering high-density areas under VFR come as a total surprise to the controllers working the area. They are termed "pop-ups" on the radar screens, and necessitate a quick attempt by the controller to contact the pop-up and vector him around and through the IFR traffic. The simple filing of a flight plan at the private pilot's airport of departure would, in some small way, warn controllers in other areas that the plane would be coming through. But even proposals to make the filing of such flight plans mandatory are beaten down by private aviation's spokesmen. It takes no more than one to two minutes for a private pilot to file a VFR flight plan. AOPA recommends to its members that they file flight plans whenever conducting a flight. But the moment talk arises of making flight plans mandatory, AOPA takes a stand against it as an unnecessary infringement on the private pilot's freedom of operation.

The training of a private pilot is geared to one simple goal, that of seeing the student pass his written and flight tests.

Even the 70 percent figure for passing the FAA test is misleading. There is no consideration of which 30 percent of the questions were answered incorrectly. The student pilot taking the test could be woefully lacking in knowledge of such critical areas as procedures when flying in control zones, radio navigation procedures, and air terminal control procedures. In other words, it's the 30 percent wrong answers that can kill you.

The written test consists of fifty questions, most of which are either the 50–50 yes or no type or multiple choice examination questions with four possible answers for each one. Many of the questions deal with FAA regulations, which prove nothing about the student's ability to pilot an airplane, although they do ascertain his capacity for memorizing regulations and rules. The specific questions are changed from time to time, but the relative ratio of areas of knowledge tested remains approximately the same from test to test. Here are some sample questions:

1. "Flight time" means the time from the moment the aircraft
    a. engine is started until it is shut down.
    b. starts to taxi until it is parked.
    c. first moves under its own power for the purpose of flight until it first comes to rest at the next point of landing (block-to-block time).
    d. First moves under its own power for the purpose of flight until the moment it lands.

2. "Large aircraft" means aircraft of more than
    a. 12,500 pounds empty weight.
    b. 12,500 pounds maximum certified takeoff weight.
    c. 12,500 pounds gross weight only when pilot and copilot are required as a minimum crew.
    d. 60 feet wing span and 25,000 pounds maximum certified takeoff weight.

3. If an applicant takes a written examination required for certification as a private or commercial pilot on January 9, and is advised that he failed, he may apply for retesting
    a. either on February 8, or after obtaining a minimum of 10 hours of additional instruction.
    b. only if 30 days have passed since the date he failed that test.
    c. only upon presenting a statement from a certified flight instructor with an appropriate category rating, certifying that he has given additional instruction to

the applicant and now considers that he is ready for retesting.

d. by observing either of the requirements as stated in (b) or (c).

4. Only when specifically authorized to do so by a Flight Standards District Office may any person act as a pilot in command of a turbojet-powered airplane who does not hold

a. a type rating for that aircraft.

b. an airline transport pilot certificate.

c. a commercial pilot certificate.

d. a Class I medical certificate.

5. The holder of a pilot certificate who has a change in permanent mailing address should notify

a. The nearest FAA General Aviation District Office either in person or by telephone as soon as possible.

b. in writing and within 30 days after the change, the FAA Airman Certification Branch, Oklahoma City, Okla.

c. The Chairman, Aeronautics Board, Washington, D.C.

d. The medical examiner at the time the holder's medical certificate is renewed.

6. Excluding the requirement applicable to airline transport pilots, a logbook or some other reliable record of flying time

a. is not necessary once a student pilot acquires a pilot certificate.

b. must be maintained only on all flying done for hire.

c. must be maintained only for that flying time submitted to document the experience requirements for any pilot certificate or rating, or to meet the recent experience requirements of Part 61, Federal Aviation Regulations.

d. must be maintained on all dual, copilot, and pilot-in-command flying.

7. A second-class medical certificate, for operations requiring a commercial pilot certificate, expires
a. at the end of the last day of the 12th month after the month in which it was issued.
b. 12 months from the date of issuance.
c. on the date of issuance 12 months after issuance.
d. at the end of the first day of the 12th month after the date of issuance.

8. Before commanding a cross-country flight, each pilot in command is required by regulations to
a. familiarize himself with all available information concerning the flight, including weather reports and fuel requirements.
b. make a preflight check to determine that the airplane is in safe operating condition, but nothing more.
c. make a preflight check and file a flight plan.
d. accomplish both (a) and (c).

9. A U.S.-certified pilot operating a foreign civil aircraft in the United States under VFR conditions
a. must file a VFR flight plan.
b. must file a VFR flight plan only if he is carrying passengers.
c. is not required by regulations to file any type of flight plan.
d. must file an IFR flight plan and conduct all flights along civil airways.

10. The operator of an airplane of less than 12,500 pounds (not operating under FAR Part 135) and of U.S. registry is involved in a landing accident in Mexico. The accident results in substantial damage to the airplane,

but no injuries to anyone. Under these circumstances, Part 320 of Safety Investigation Regulations

a. does not require the operator to notify either the Federal Aviation Administration or the NTSB since the accident occurred outside the continental limits of the United States.

b. requires the operator to submit a report to the nearest Bureau of Safety Field Office of the NTSB within 10 days.

c. requires the operator to notify the NTSB immediately and submit a report within 10 days to the nearest FAA Flight Standards District Office.

d. requires the operator to notify the closest U.S. consular official immediately and to submit a report to him within 7 days.

11. Damage incurred during the operation of an aircraft of more than 12,500 pounds must be reported

a. only if repairs are reasonably estimated to cost $300 or more.

b. if major repair or replacement of the affected component would normally be required.

c. only if fire in flight was the primary cause of the damage.

d. only for operations conducted under the provisions of FAR Part 135 (Air Taxi Operators and Commercial Operators of Small Aircraft).

12. The NTSB must be notified immediately of incidents which involve

a. unwanted or asymmetrical thrust reverse.

b. rapid decompression.

c. in-flight fire.

d. engine failure.

The following are other types of question:

1. Must medical certificates be carried on the person while piloting an aircraft?

2. What class medical certificate must an applicant hold if he is to be eligible for a commercial pilot certificate? (Fill-in answer required.)

3. For how long a period are private and commercial pilot certificates valid? (Fill-in answer required.)

4. May a certified pilot, who meets recent experience requirements in a small, single-engine land airplane, fly as pilot-in-command of all airplanes in this class?

5. May civilian pilots operate civil aircraft in formation flight?

6. May a non-instrument-rated pilot operate an aircraft in a positive control area?

7. Is it mandatory that the pilot keep his seat belt fastened while at the controls of an airplane?

8. May an aircraft be operated between sunset and sunrise without lighted position lights?

Questions such as these, when considered against the task of flying an aircraft in today's aviation medium, are irrelevant and useless. There are, of course, other questions on the FAA written test that relate directly to aircraft operation. There is also an exercise in which the student must plot a cross-country flight, using the navigational techniques he's been taught in training. In my case, I plotted my cross-country trip and, through miscalculation, ran out of gas somewhere over Kentucky. I passed anyway.

I discussed the written test with Dr. Strickler and Lovering of the FAA.

QUESTION: Isn't it true that it's very easy to pass the written test and become a private pilot?

STRICKLER: Right. The superman theory is a bunch of hogwash.

QUESTION: Why is a student pilot allowed to pass the

written test when he misses 30 percent of the questions? That 30 percent can kill him, and a lot of other people, can't it?

LOVERING: I agree that in operating any kind of machine, 30 percent gap in knowledge can kill you—in an airplane, car, tank, bus, tractor—and we recognize this in the FAA. But when an individual takes his examination and gets a 70 percent score, he is advised of his areas of weakness. So this gives him a chance to go back and bone up on those areas in which he's weak.

QUESTION: How many go back and bone up?

LOVERING: Well, there has to be some motivation, some self-motivation.

Such motivation is not abundantly evident. There are, without doubt, many who take their flying seriously and work to perfect their proficiency. But, it would seem, a far greater number go on flying without any serious attempts to upgrade themselves.

AOPA and the aircraft manufacturers constantly labor to make private flying easy for more participants. Both groups actively fight any mandatory recertification proposals.

"What we are after and what we want is a transportation system in which the most limited individual can participate safely." Robert Monroe, AOPA's congressional liaison and the only registered lobbyist in the association, told me this during an interview. "It must not be so demanding that it requires a high degree of training or expertise to participate."

The goal of which Monroe speaks is honorable and ideal. But it is hardly a realistic one when considered in light of aviation's demands and growing sophistication. Monroe acknowledged to me that the airlines have extremely high standards. Cockpit crews consist of two or three people to cope with the intricacies and complexities of flying swift aircraft in crowded skies. Safety equipment alone aboard airline aircraft runs to as much as one million per jet plane. The critics of private aviation often ask whether it is unreasonable to expect others sharing the airspace with airline crews and passengers to upgrade their proficiency and the capability of their aircraft in the interest of safety. As far as Max Karant of AOPA is concerned, nothing of a regulatory nature should be done until after the fact. How horrendous this *fact* must be before action is not specified. Congressman Rosenthal of Queens, New York, has stated, "Nothing will be done until a drunken seventeen-year-old kid in a private plane flying over Brooklyn smacks into an airline jet loaded with people."

"We've got pilots flying around here who don't have any business doing half the things they do," says Karant. "I'll never deny this. All I can say is, look, fella, these people are a cross section of the American populace—in many ways they are better economically and so on—but they are still a cross section of the American people and until they do something that is horrendous, leave 'em alone!"

AOPA and the aircraft manufacturers have devoted themselves to seeing that private pilots are left alone. AOPA's members have gotten their money's worth. Nowhere in the world are private pilots more left alone than in America. This freedom caused Jerry Hulse, the popular travel writer of the *Los Angeles Times*, to devote his entire column of October 1, 1967, to the problem. Hulse wrote: "Every time I get caught in an overcast over some big city I can't help wondering if some joker in a private airplane isn't up there, too. Alongside us, maybe. Or worse yet, in front of us. He's [the airline pilot] flown thousands of hours under practically every condition imaginable. He's prepared for practically any eventuality. But there's damn little he or anyone else can do if some clown in a private airplane darts in his way over a major airport."

Congressman Rosenthal has also commented on the dangers of the "free" private pilot. He stated at a news conference in

1968, "The rights of 99 percent of the public have been ignored in favor of scantily equipped small planes piloted by amateurs who insist on their right to fly anywhere."

AOPA has defended its position against any recertification program by warning the FAA of the supposed economic consequences. The May, 1968, issue of *The Pilot* said, "The potential danger to the entire general aviation industry posed by the proposed rules changes would be reflected in a substantial increase in the cost of private flying. Thousands of private pilots would stop flying, FBO's [fixed base operators] therefore would lose business, aircraft production would have to be cut back and used aircraft would become a glut on the market."

Max Karant is a brusque and outspoken man. He has little regard for the moderating forces creeping into private aviation. Highly respected by many in the industry and an experienced and highly proficient pilot, Karant has been dedicated to improved safety in aviation. But he has also proved himself to be a major stumbling block in the way of any safety legislation and regulation. There are those who feel that Karant really doesn't *feel* as bullish as he *talks*.

"Max is in a box," an airline acquaintance told me. "He's got a membership of about 150,000 private pilots who want action for their nineteen dollars a year dues. Max and AOPA have to give them action."

Whether AOPA and Karant take some of their stands in the interest of pleasing and increasing the membership is speculative. Karant denies it, as does Robert Monroe. And it is true that an increasing number of AOPA members feel only a moderating position will accomplish anything in the current struggle for aviation power. These members are not weak, but they realize that as AOPA becomes more extreme in its position, it becomes more vulnerable to criticism and potential defeat. The shrill cries of AOPA are losing effectiveness. After a time, you simply become weary of being yelled at.

The moderates in AOPA comprise a small percentage of

the membership. The association does, indeed, feel its back pressed against a wall. The membership insists that the principle of freedom of flight through the nation's navigable airspace is precious and must be maintained. AOPA mirrors this position.

I asked Karant why private aviation insisted on having equal and free rights to such airports as LaGuardia and Kennedy when their very operations there delay and endanger many people.

KARANT: For the same reason we want to drive on the streets of New York.

REPORTER: For the principle of it.

KARANT: It's more than the principle of it. The principle of it is important, of course. I must have the right to go there [LaGuardia or Kennedy airports]. They must be open to me.

As with the goal of making flying easy enough for everyone with minimum training and ability to participate, Karant's principle of free access to all airports is ideal. No one would deny that, if conditions were such that all pilots could use all airports equally and safely, this would provide the ideal aviation environment. But in the case of high-density hub areas it is impossible. Standing on principle becomes academic and naïve in the face of the problem.

The frustration of trying to find someone in the FAA willing to speak of the issue is considerable. It is understandable that those responsible for the condition in the first place would be unwilling to admit openly a problem exists. I mentioned to Ralph Lovering that I felt there were a number of incompetent private pilots.

"Can you prove it?" he replied.

I brought up the thousands of accidents each year in which the private pilot is cited as a causal or the causal factor.

"What's the answer?" Lovering asked. "Regulation? Can we regulate judgment in the cockpit?"

My frustration was beginning to develop.

"What I'm saying, Mr. Lovering, is that if a training level is high enough and a man has met the high standards and continues to meet those high standards through periodic checks on him, and then displays a lack of judgment in a situation, I forgive him in that error. It is the human factor at play. You cannot regulate against that. But if the training is, to begin with, inadequate and incapable of preparing the man for operating in the medium with which he is dealing, and nothing is ever done to upgrade that training, then I become concerned."

Lovering considered my statement. "Let's be specific," he said. "Do you have any cases in mind? Do you have any cases you can recall that would bear out this premise you're making here today?"

I gave him all the examples. I mentioned the lack of regulations concerning recertification. I brought up my being able to rent an airplane after such a long period of not flying. I cited the FAA's own statistics, which indicate that over 80 percent of private aviation accidents are due to pilot error and/or bad jugment. I mentioned the increasing number of "saves" by FAA controllers each year. And I mentioned the drinking and flying problem.

Lovering sat back and spoke softly.

"Let's say we've changed chairs, Mr. Bain, and you are in the Federal Aviation Administration. Knowing what you know and feeling the way you do and under the existing laws and statutes, let's say you are the chairman of the regulatory council—you have the power to write the laws. What kind of laws would you write?"

We discussed the areas in which I felt new regulation was needed. During the conversation, Dr. Strickler asked if I had any firm statistics on how many lives would be saved if new regulations were passed. My face must have reflected my feelings about this kind of logic because he quickly added that such statistics shouldn't be the only criteria for new regulations.

Lovering brought up a program of which he was especially proud.

"Do you have a Blue Seal Certificate?" he asked me. "Does your private pilot's license have a little blue seal on it?" We looked at my license and found it did not have any little blue seal. "Well," he continued, "since you received your license, the FAA has put in a rule that says—I believe it went into effect in 1960—that all pilots shall receive a certain amount of instrument training. This is important. Terribly important. In 1956 or 1957 or 1958, we recognized that weather was the major cause of fatal accidents. So a concerted effort was put into that area. After much strain and pain in working with the public, the regulations were changed to specify that before you were issued a pilot's license, one of the requisites would be that you could control an aircraft manually—keep that word manually in mind—by reference to instruments. This was given in training and as part of the flight test. So everyone who was issued a certificate was issued a blue seal. This was to stimulate people such as yourself who received a certificate earlier than 1960 to come back for re-certification and say, 'Mr. Inspector, how do I get my little blue seal?'

"I would say that over 70 percent of these people came back and got their blue seal on their license. They came back in and said they wanted this little seal. They'd say they were sitting in their friend's house the other night and noticed their friend had this little blue seal on his license. How come I'm different? AOPA jumped on the bandwagon and have what they call a blue seal clinic. There are very few people flying today who do not have their little blue seal. This was a motivation device given to the individuals even if only for their pride. I've got this blue seal, they could then say. This has done a lot to bring the pilot up to a level of high standards, and it did take a reissuance of the certificate and another flight test. It did take a rule to put in this blue seal concept. We've gone one step farther. We've come to realize that the weakest link in the private licensing system is the flight instructor. So today, we have a little gold seal that may be issued to the flight instructor who will come in and reprove his competence after he has done a certain amount of training."

To AOPA, it would seem, just about every proposal made by the FAA that affects private aviation is part of an airline plot to do away with the private plane and pilot. When the recertification proposal was up in the air in 1968, AOPA ended another of its articles in *The Pilot* with, "FAA's new bid to add another layer to the regulatory blanket is made in the name of air safety. But that claim is far from substantiated. And the approach, presumably suggested by a shot from the hip of air carrier [airline] interests is one that might easily backfire to the detriment of the entire U.S. civil aviation industry."

The fact is, the recertification proposals have been offered with the hope that, by insuring a better grade of private pilot in the air, the danger to others would be cut down. They have been proposed hopefully to protect the private pilot from himself, something the statistics would indicate he isn't very adroit at accomplishing himself, and to make the aviation system a better one for all its users. All these FAA proposals, including such basic ones as that which would prohibit a pilot from drinking before and during the piloting of an airplane, have met strong and concerted opposition. Private aviation makes its voice heard and its weight felt against the rule changes, and in most instances the proposal becomes just another docket in the burgeoning files of defeated FAA proposed rule changes. All of this points vividly to the unfortunate fact that air safety for everyone is not necessarily the goal and posture of private aviation.

"We have an awful lot of AOPA people in FAA headquarters," Max Karant told me. "They oppose us publicly, and then they privately say, 'Don't let up and here's the next thing you ought to do.' " In this view, the FAA appears to be controlled by outside (and inside) forces with special interests and selfish, self-serving goals that are alien to the responsibility given the FAA.

Edward Stimpson is a congressional liaison man for the FAA. It is his job to keep in touch with the Congress and provide a flow of information between the FAA and the Hill. Stimpson has said, "We've got AOPA and NBAA and the Airport Operator's Council and so on, but the poor American traveling public whom we're out to protect in the first place really isn't heard from."

Stimpson also referred to the carefully plotted and aggressively carried out campaigns of private aviation to influence rule making. "When you consider the fact that general aviation mail is stimulated by such associations as AOPA, then, if you were to take a count of the letters that come in whenever a rule change is proposed, you'd find it running highly in favor of general aviation's side of things. It's like the hearings we held recently on the high-density issue. We had something like three thousand comments received for the docket and practically every one of them was against the rule."

In 1967, the FAA brought 2,116 actions against individual pilots. Of these, 628 resulted in civil penalties in which a fine was paid, no criminal record resulted, and no action was taken against the pilot's right to fly unhindered. Nine hundred sixty-six of these actions resulted in suspension of the pilot's license for a specified period of time, with full restoration of the flying privilege, and 222 licenses were revoked. Three hundred resulted in no action of any kind. Those pilots who had their licenses revoked could appeal to the NTSB. It should be noted that none of the 1967 actions against pilots were brought posthumously, but were above and beyond the fatalities caused by pilot error. By taking the accidents of 1967 attributed to pilot error and/or lack of judgment, and adding that figure to both the number of FAA actions against individual pilots in the same year and the number of pilots "saved" by FAA ground controllers, you have almost eleven thousand cases of *bad piloting*, or roughly thirty a day.

The situation is not destined to improve. The danger grows in simple proportion to the increase in the number of people training for and receiving their private pilot's certificates. Each year finds more and more citizens going through the training mill and emerging as qualified pilots, qualified under present minimum standards established by the FAA. There are now approximately 550,000 licensed pilots; 525,000 of, them are non-airline pilots. The number of pilots increases each year at a rate of about 13 percent, with student pilots increasing at an even faster rate. In 1968, approximately 150,000 student pilot certificates were issued by the FAA. And an increasing number of these students will not only learn to fly from a civilian flight instructor, but will be certified as meeting the minimum FAA standards by the same private flight instructor, without any validation by an FAA inspector.

There are now 1,300 private flight instructors and/or schools in the United States that are authorized by the FAA to certify their students. It can be fairly assumed that the great majority of these instructors and schools are honest and dedicated to turning out pilots who do, in fact, meet the FAA standards for private pilots. And it is equally fair to assume that a certain percentage will abuse their authorization.

The authorization of private individuals to accomplish the FAA's work came about when the agency admitted that it could no longer keep up with aviation's growth. This was especially true with private aviation.

"The general aviation industry has expanded so rapidly in the past five years—and the prediction for growth is even more astounding—that there is no possible way we in government can do the work from a government employee standpoint. We simply had to give this authority over to the industry." That was Ralph Lovering of the FAA commenting in the summer of 1968 in response to my questions about the private instructor situation. I'd found it difficult to accept that the FAA, the agency charged with air safety, would allow thousands of private instructors to validate their own students. An indentical situation exists in aircraft maintenance. Aircraft mechanics repair airplanes and then pass on their own work without any FAA inspection.

Lovering went on to say, "We hope to go a lot farther in this area of designating the industry. For example, Piper, Beech, and Cessna have what we call a delegated option to certificate their own new aircraft. As it rolls out the door, he [the manufacturer] puts a certificate on it for the FAA."

QUESTION: Isn't there a risk of unscrupulous people operating under this delegating system, especially in the areas of flight instruction and aircraft repair?

LOVERING: Certainly. We always have cases where there is an individual who'll sell a ticket [license] for five, ten, fifteen, whatever the market will bear. But as soon as we're aware of this, he is shut off, but fast.

QUESTION: Isn't that shutting the barn door after the horse is gone?

LOVERING: Sure. But we have the ability under the Federal Aviation Act to go back to any one of the students he's certified and retest him.

The FAA has done little going back to retest students. It wasn't until 1968 that it began cracking down on airmen who cheated on the written exams. It announced in a press release in October, 1968, that investigations into irregularities in the use of airman examinations had led to at least twenty-five violation actions against individuals. Some of these violations involved the falsifying of airman certification records by FAA-authorized flight instructors. One case concerned a publisher of airman training manuals who, it was alleged, had illegally obtained and utilized FAA written examinations. The FAA managed to gain an injunction against the publisher who also happened to own and operate a flight training school.

Flight training schools are bulging with new student pilots. The manufacturers have engaged in impressive and effective campaigns to entice people into the air. FAA-designated flight schools and instructors are becoming increasingly busy, a condition conducive to more hurried flight training and the desire to push the students through as fast as possible to make way for a new batch. Many schools guarantee a pilot's license for a set sum of money; economic necessity dictates a need for these schools to pass a student through training and on to his license with all possible haste. In short, the entire system is not one designed to foster quality instruction and rigorous and demanding testing.

The FAA has always been willing to hold the hands of the inexperienced and incapable pilot. It recently established a trial situation in which air traffic controllers would speak more slowly and use lay terms for any pilot indicating to them that he was inexperienced. The experiment was scrapped, much to the relief of both airline pilots, who had to wait while the slow radio talk went on, and the controllers, who found it trying and annoying.

Recalling the experiment, Walter A. Jensen, assistant vice-president of operations and engineering for the Air Transport Association (ATA), commented, "That experiment was a failure and I'm glad it was. You can't hold the hands of the inexperienced in such a sophisticated medium as aviation."

Today, the FAA sits in an unenviable position. It is caught between the two responsibilities given it by the Federal Aviation Act of 1958, namely, to insure air safety and, at the same time, promote the growth of civil aviation and insure free access to all airspace. These two responsibilities have become incompatible. The FAA cannot condone and foster mediocre pilots and minimum standards for pilots and still assure a reasonable level of safety to the hundreds of millions of airline passengers. Section 104 of the Federal Aviation Act, quoted at the very beginning of this book, has become outdated and unworkable in the span of eleven years. The rights of a few can no longer be preserved in their entirety when the rights of a mass traveling public are denied in their favor. This is the position of one side in the aviation conflict. The other side, private aviation and its associations, led by AOPA, feels that the rights of the individual private aviator must take priority. Max Karant of AOPA summed it up when he said, "The reason we're so sensitive is that we've been treated like second-class citizens for so long that we got where we were taking it for granted. We'd even walk to the back of the bus and sit on separate but equal toilets. But no more! We have a hell of a big industry that's predicated on the fact that people are using planes just like they use their automobiles. For travel. Business. Pleasure. Just travel. And that has to be protected at all costs."

What are the costs? Evidently, Urbana and Hendersonville and other midair collisions have not been sufficient payment.

CHAPTER FOUR

The Silent Passenger

The commercial airlines are public carriers, regulated by law, open to all. Last year they carried 130-million passengers. They are a vital part of the national transportation system. Where limited airport facilities necessitate a choice, common carriers should have preference over private planes. Delay in making that choice is an invitation to disaster.

Editorial
New York Times
August 13, 1968

The summer of 1968 will go down in history as one of extreme frustration for the nation's air travelers. Delays during the peak summer months were staggering. The multitude of airline passengers who spent millions of hours circling above waiting to land, or waiting on the ground eager to take off, finally became aware of the crisis in this nation's aviation industry. They discovered that the crisis was a facts-and-figures reality, a time-consuming, money-grabbing, and potentially life-taking dilemma.

During one day in July, more than twenty thousand passengers on two hundred flights were delayed at Kennedy Airport. Most of these flights were delayed an hour or more. The FAA estimates that airline passengers lost over seven million man-hours in 1968 due to delays, at a cost to the passengers of $300 million in lost time. These delays occurred mostly at the major hub areas of the country. New York and its three major airports—LaGuardia, Kennedy, and Newark—suffered most from the congestion. Sam Saint, a veteran American Airlines pilot, indicated the severity of the problem when he commented, "Before July of 1968, you could expect anywhere from a twenty-five to a forty-minute delay out of Kennedy. But once things really got bad, we started figuring on delays of two hours and more."

By July of 1968, aircraft delays in the New York area were averaging one hundred minutes. During the last week in July, it was not uncommon for aircraft to sit on the ground and wait three hours to be given takeoff clearance. Oscar Bakke, acting deputy administrator of the FAA during the summer of 1968, testified about conditions in the New York area at emergency hearings called by the House of Subcommittee of the Committee on Government Operations on August 1. He used one day at LaGuardia to illustrate how large the congestion problem had grown.

"At LaGuardia this week—I think it was Tuesday—we had a situation in which everything simply stopped," Bakke told the committee. "For a period of approximately two hours, because of flow restrictions in the en route facility, aircraft were moving out at a slow rate. The tower was compelled to keep aircraft at the gate positions. As aircraft continued to land, they were stopped at the ramp, unable to move into the gate positions. Soon, the taxiways leading to the ramp were congested. And finally, for a period of about two hours, all traffic into LaGuardia was stopped, simply because there was no longer physical room at the airport to accommodate any additional aircraft. This is what we mean when we say that delay ultimately reaches infinity. With that kind of pressure, it comes completely to a halt."

It was Bakke who had forecast a saturation of the New York airports by 1968. In June, 1967, he told the Wings Club of New York, a club made up of members from the aviation community, "The present airport configuration in the New York metropolitan area will be saturated for all practical purposes before the end of 1968." Sadly, Bakke was one of only a handful of agency and congressional officials who were looking ahead.

The passengers, who have suffered and will suffer from aviation's ills, began complaining about delay. But their complaints were private, voiced at home to their wives and in the office to business associates. Airline ticket agents bore some of their wrath, as did stewardesses and waitresses at airport coffee shops and bars. Such passenger ire did not reach Washington, where the FAA and Congress must make decisions affecting the airline passenger, his convenience and safety. The airlines, as corporate entities, are aware of their passengers' needs, and much of their activity would conceivably result in improvement of the passenger's lot. When the airlines speak, however, they are viewed by private aviation as profit-greedy corporations with shareholders demanding a greater return for their investment. There is an element of truth in this, of course, but it is in the public interest, to say nothing of the passenger's interest, to have a healthy commercial aviation system in which reasonable profits are realized. Fares can be lowered only when profits are gained. Deficits in airline operations result in government-approved fare increases, the most recent put into effect in March, 1969. However, the size of the nation's airline industry makes it suspect when it offers proposals and demands to the federal government. Consequently, its voice is diluted and vulnerable to attack by the private aviation sector.

It is the airline passenger who must be heard. He has no axe to grind except that of wanting efficient and safe air travel. But he has been the silent voice.

The economic impact of congestion on the airlines is considerable. The individual lines are already caught in a fiscal vise because of the need for new equipment, rising labor costs, and growing competitive spirit within the industry. The purchase of new aircraft to accommodate the increase in passenger travel will cost the nation's domestic airlines about $10.5 billion by 1979. This new equipment is the result of demand exceeding supply. In 1962, only 10 percent of the population had ever been up in an airplane. By 1967, that figure had risen to 42 percent. The jet set was no longer composed of a small number of the wealthy; it included everyone.

According to CAB figures, it costs an airline an average of $5.50 per minute of delay. Delays cost the nation's airlines in excess of $80 million in 1968, double what it cost them for delays in 1964. Fuel consumption, crew overtime pay, and inefficient aircraft utilization account for most of these costs, all of which are passed on to the passenger in one form or another.

The economics of air traffic congestion affect the public, both flying and nonflying, in ways other than increased or stagnant fares. One example of this is the economic impact upon communities that depend on a viable and dynamic system of public air transportation. Again using the New York area as an example, it becomes evident that congestion begins to erode the economic base and growth of an area. For the first time in Kennedy Airport's twenty-year history, domestic travel declined over the previous year. Kennedy was once the gateway to Europe, but travel agencies are now routing clients to overseas destinations via other domestic terminal areas, notably Philadelphia and Boston. Toronto and Montreal have also begun to get increased passenger traffic that ordinarily would have funneled through Kennedy, in New York. The Ford Motor Company has suggested to its thousands of employees that they detour around New York whenever possible.

The federal government has begun taking measures against traffic into New York. The CAB recently authorized Northeast Airlines to begin flying between New England and the Midwest, provided the airline skipped New York with these new flights. The CAB is also considering the establishment of direct routes to Europe from a number of East Coast cities in an attempt to bypass New York's congestion. And the FAA has instituted plans that limit the number of flight operations in and out of New York's three airports, resulting in a drop in service and scheduling available to the population of the area. Already, Northeast Airlines has canceled its hourly service between New York and Boston because of the economic squeeze of congestion. Eastern announced it would no longer be able to operate its convenient shuttle service between New York and Boston-Washington under the FAA's proposed cuts in operations, scheduled for the summer of 1969. And Pan American has applied for overseas service from Hartford, Connecticut, to try to avoid New York's traffic pileup.

As the flow of travelers through New York decreases, many segments of the area's economy are affected. R. Dixon Speas Associates, management consultants specializing in airline problems, estimate the potential loss to the New York area will reach $200 million by 1975 if the congestion isn't alleviated. The bulk of this loss will be in airline-airport employee wages—$162 million. The balance will be the loss of tourist spending. While New York has been hardest hit, it is no more than indicative of what other metropolitan hub areas face. Queens Congressman Benjamin Rosenthal has stated, "The aviation problems at New York are not New York's alone. They are national problems, both in their immediate effects on delays in other areas and in their imminent parallels at airports serving all of America's cities." Rosenthal's analysis is accurate. When one airport becomes saturated, it affects flights all over the country, and the world. Flights bound for the destination airport must enter holding patterns until the congestion eases; in New York's case, flights heading there stack up as far west as Denver, and others never leave the ground at their departure airports.

David D. Thomas, the last FAA administrator during President Johnson's Administration, said in November, 1968, "The problems of JFK and O'Hare today could be those of Wichita or Nashville tomorrow."

Summer 1968 made many more people aware of the aviation crisis. It came to a head when two factors merged. One was the peak vacation rush, particularly to Europe. The other was the decision of the newly formed air traffic controller organization, the Professional Air Traffic Controllers Organization (PATCO) to begin regulating aircraft "by the book." Until the time of their decision, controllers had pushed far beyond the FAA limits stipulated as safe and reasonable. They'd done this with the tacit approval of the FAA. Everyone was aware that this stretching of the rules caused an unsafe situation. But in the midst of increasing air traffic and increasing passenger demand, the FAA was content to allow the controllers to handle more aircraft by shrinking the separation distance normally required for these aircraft.

The rules state that planes must be separated by three miles when within forty miles of an airport, and by five miles farther from the terminal area. The rules also dictate procedures for aircraft leaving airport areas. Before the controller "slowdown," the controllers had stretched the rules and allowed aircraft to come closer together in flight to increase the usage of the airspace, and allowed aircraft to use direct, shortcut takeoff runways and deviate from standard patterns when leaving the area. Then, to dramatize PATCO's demands for more help and better equipment, the controllers went back to strict interpretation of the rules. The result was chaos. Even with a bending of the rules, delays had been substantial at the major hubs. With a literal interpretation of the FAA rules, the situation became intolerable. In one twenty-four-hour period in the New York area, 1,927 aircraft were delayed, some as long as three hours.

The initial reaction of the public was to point an accusing finger at the controllers for their actions. But as the story became better known, the public began to view the controllers' position more sympathetically. As the responsibilities of the controllers' job became known and publicized, the public began to feel the proper appreciation for these overworked men whose every move could result in disaster. The pressures of their job had not been recognized before by the public. Working with antiquated radar equipment that broke down at frequent intervals, substantially understaffed at each control center, the air traffic controllers were working too many hours, handling too many aircraft at one time, and, in general, being subjected to pressure beyond reasonable and prudent limits.

In the crush of congestion, the FAA made a six-day week mandatory and canceled many vacations.

Ideally, the controller should handle five or six aircraft at a time. Until the slowdown, he was called upon to handle as many as thirty simultaneously, each plane to be deftly directed to avoid collision and without any margin for error.

Heart attacks on the job increased. More and more controllers were ordered by their doctors to go on tranquilizers and remain at home. The taking of any drugs or alcohol within eight hours of a man's shift is strictly forbidden by FAA regulations. "On pills—day off" became a common phrase in employee records.

PATCO acted. At its first convention, held in Chicago in June, 1968, it was decided that a return to the rule book was the only way to make the government and the public aware of the air traffic crisis. Initially, the FAA disapproved of the action and openly criticized the controllers. But as public sympathy swung around in the men's favor, the FAA began to shift gears and adopted a new position. The FAA used PATCO's action to dramatize the agency's need for increased budgets from Congress. To an extent, the strategy worked. Congress did appropriate an emergency fund to allow the FAA to hire more controllers and to train new men entering the field. This was a step in the right direction, but it never should have become necessary. In 1967, the Flight Safety Foundation, an independent organization dedicated to studying and solving aviation problems, had offered to make a study of the airport/airways system and to make recommendations toward solutions. The FAA declined the offer.

"There is no problem," an FAA spokesman said. "If there is, we'll solve it in the house."

This head-in-the-sand philosophy on the part of the FAA was still evident in 1968. During an interview with Ralph Lovering in September of that year, I pressed the point that additional regulation over private aviation was necessary in the face of congestion and delay at hub areas. At one point during this discussion, Lovering rose from his chair, walked to the window that looks out from the top of the Department of Transportation Building, and opened the blinds.

"Come here," he said. I went and stood at his side.

"Look out there," he said. "Do you see any aircraft out there?"

I looked. It was 10:30 on a weekday morning. The sky was blue and the visibility unlimited.

"No, not at the moment," I answered.

"Look at all that airspace," Lovering continued. "Do you think that's unmanageable? How many aircraft can you count out there? I defy you to look around with your eyes and see them [airplanes]."

Had PATCO, and the controllers it represents, not come forward as it did to vividly display the inadequacies of aviation in 1968, Congress might still be laboring under the FAA's impression that if you can't see airplanes in the sky, over Washington, at 10:30 on a weekday morning, from your office window, there is no problem.

Private aviation interests made good use of the summer of 1968 to strengthen their own position. They pointed to what was now public admission by the FAA that the ATC system was inadequate and that controllers were understaffed and overworked. And they said, "Look, there's the problem. Don't talk about putting us under more control. The system can't control what's there already."

Skilled in matters of industry debate, AOPA stopped there in its argument. But two further questions were put to it by the rest of the industry.

1. Until the system is improved, and its capability increased, will you back off and allow the commercial airlines and their millions of passengers to have some sort of priority at the congested, high-density terminal areas?

2. When the system is improved and expanded, will you accept the safety need for all aircraft operating in the high-density control areas to be properly equipped and to be piloted by people with increased knowledge, training, and experience?

Private aviation's answer to both questions was a resounding "NO!" The industry repeated its philosophy of freedom for all in the airspace. It insisted that to require higher skills and better-equipped aircraft would place an unwarranted financial burden on private pilots. Private aviation became even more rigid in its stands. AOPA had always insisted that its primary objection to being excluded from major airports was that no suitable smaller airports were available in those areas. There was a great deal of validity to this position, enough so that airline spokesmen and Congress repeatedly called for improved satellite airports in metropolitan hub areas. Pan American responded by proposing to take over Teterboro and Republic airports in the New York area and invest twenty million dollars in improvements. Both airports would be operated solely for private aviation aircraft. Pan Am's motives were clearly stated. It hoped that by providing superior facilities for private aviation aircraft, the operators of these aircraft would be enticed away from Kennedy, La-Guardia, and Newark.

Based upon the past statements of private aviation, Pan American officials expected that their plan and proposal would be welcomed. However, before the CAB had concluded its hearings on the proposal (Pan Am needed CAB approval to enter into a business venture outside the line's primary mission of public carrier), AOPA came out strongly against the Teterboro and Republic project. Initially, AOPA had given tacit approval of the concept. But subsequent editorials in *The Pilot* condemned Pan Am and asked the CAB to rule against the airline. AOPA claimed that to go ahead with the plans would constitute an antitrust situation for Pan Am. It also questioned Pan Am's motives as a major airline already engaged in conflict with private aviation. Could such an enemy truly have the best interests of private aviation at heart? AOPA thought not.

Private aviation's refusal to accept improved airports for its own use in metropolitan areas resulted in sustained and increased pressure on the major hub airports. The airlines, speaking through the Air Transport Association, urged that a priority system at high-density airports to put into effect in 1968. They asked that their operations, and their passengers, be given preference when and where congestion necessitated a choice. The nation's press, for the most part, agreed.

The *Journal of Commerce* said, in a July 26, 1968, editorial, "If the public would be better off by having private craft use of major airports restricted to off hours or eliminated entirely, then by all means such a decision should be made."

The *Washington Star* said in an editorial on August 4, 1968, "Measures like a priority system for passenger jets are vital."

The *New York Daily News* editorialized on September 6, 1968, "The FAA proposes to shoulder a lot of small private plane traffic to smaller airports. . . This plan is drawing the expected squawks . . . but we can see nothing for it except to override those objections. You can hardly bar an ocean liner from a North River Dock to let two or three rowboats or pint-sized yachts tie up there."

The *Wall Street Journal* said on September 23, 1968, "For the moment, the FAA idea of priority for the airlines at crowded ports probably is essential; the convenience of the greatest number—airline passengers—should get precedence."

The *New York Times* said on August 20, 1968, "While the emergency persists, drastic measures must be taken to cope with it, even at the cost of ending the time-honored practice that all aircraft, large or small, must be treated on a first-come, first-served basis."

Private aviation fought back. It repeatedly quoted Section 104 of the 1958 Federal Aviation Act. It charged "persecution." And it undertook an aggressive campaign with its members to bring weight to bear on Congress and the FAA.

The FAA, a proverbial political football, sat placidly in the middle of the fray. On one hand, there was the Department of Transportation, and even President Lyndon Johnson himself, asking for reason in the decision-making process. On September 20, 1967, the President had written Alan S. Boyd, secretary of transportation, about his feelings on the financing of improvements to ATC. His letter was introduced into the June, 1968, hearings on the Airport Development Act, held by the Aviation Subcommittee of the Senate Committee on Commerce. In the letter, Johnson stated:

"It is apparent that the rapid growth of commercial and private flying is creating demands for substantial expansion and improvement in the Nation's air traffic control system. The Federal government is the manager of this system. System improvements will, therefore, require large additional outlays of Federal funds for investment and operations. Those who will benefit most from such expenditures, the aviation industry and the flying public, should pay their fair share of the costs of the system needed to handle the increase in air traffic while maintaining a high level of safety. I do not believe the general taxpayer should be asked to shoulder this burden."

The President's letter was not received kindly by private aviation. Although he did not specify preference for the airline position, the President did touch upon a crucial factor in the aviation crisis—"should pay their *fair share*" is the key phrase, for despite private aviation's various claims that it had been paying an appropriate share of the airways/airports cost, the figures tell a different tale. (The entire financial question is studied closely in a subsequent chapter.) The President's letter was cause for great concern in the private aviation sector.

Even more disheartening was the testimony of Secretary Boyd before that same Senate committee. Boyd said, "The federal government has greater interest in promoting the efficiency of the common carrier system of air transportation than it does in promoting private air transportation and, where a choice must be made, the common carrier system will receive preference: The federal government must insure that the nation has and maintains a safe, efficient, convenient, and economical system of common carriage by air. Under no circumstances can we allow the quality of that system to deteriorate. Within the limits of available funds, and taking into account the source of the revenues supporting the system, our objective will be to build a system which maximizes safety and efficiency for all users."

Boyd's comments triggered a number of articles and editorials written for *The Pilot*. One editorial was titled "Sellout." In it, AOPA charged that "Mr. Boyd has so misused his public position that he no longer warrants the respect that should be due cabinet-level officials." AOPA termed Boyd a "dangerous man" in another editorial. From private aviation's point of view, Secretary Boyd was dangerous. His principal strength, and the resulting threat to private aviation, was that he headed a new agency in Washington. The Department of Transportation (DOT) had been established on March 1, 1967, to attempt to bring all the nation's transportation problems under one roof, and to attempt to view individual modes of transportation in a more total framework. It had become evident that increasing the capacity of air transportation would be a wasted effort unless linking ground transportation, rail and bus services, and highway capacity were also increased. Until the DOT came into being, no central transportation agency had existed.

By August, 1968, AOPA was well into its attack on DOT. An article in *The Pilot* that month was titled "We've Had Enough of DOT." A subheadline read, "Apparent attempts of Department of Transportation to tax and regulate general aviation into a stage of regression led to demand by AOPA President that FAA be reestablished as an independent Federal agency."

Private aviation was beginning to long for the good old days when its relationship with the FAA was cozy and comfortable. It still was, to a lesser extent, but this new menace, DOT, now reviewed FAA decisions. With DOT's concern for the masses, the FAA was hard pressed to justify decisions made in favor of private aviation.

The high-density summer of 1968 brought all these elements into the open. The mood of both Congress and the Administration seemed to be one of concern for the traveling public and, by natural extension, sympathy for the airline position. AOPA launched an aggressive and concerted drive to regain some of its lost ground. The primary tool in this drive, as in other campaigns, was its membership, always willing to carry AOPA's messages to the nation's elected officials.

AOPA is not registered as a lobbying organization. Its only registered lobbyist is Robert Monroe, who is one of hundreds of individuals or organizations registered as paid lobbyists in Washington. In its pure and honorable sense, lobbying is the honest attempt by groups or individuals to influence the lawmakers in matters of deep concern to the groups or individuals. Unfortunately, lobbying can also become a selfish grab for power, too often conducted by powerful self-interest groups with substantial economic stakes in the outcome of legislation.

Lobbyists must register only when they are attempting to influence a specific piece of legislation. Attempts to influence any of the federal regulatory agencies, such as the FAA, do not require registration or reporting. A general day-by-day lobbying campaign is not subject to regulation under a 1946 act unless a specific piece of legislation is involved.

Consequently, AOPA is able to remain outside Washington's official lobbying circles. Monroe registers only as a matter of record; he told me he does so simply because the act is there and, to some people, the failure to register creates an adverse image. It is Monroe's conviction that, under the strict interpretation of the lobby act, neither he nor AOPA would be required to register.

Registered lobbying groups or individuals are required to submit quarterly reports on expenditures directly related to lobbying activity. In 1967, 280 groups reported spending $4.7 million for lobbying. AOPA reported spending nothing, despite the fact that much of its energy and attention are devoted to influencing legislation and rule making. Legally, and under the lobbying act's structure, AOPA and Monroe are sound.

In 1967, AOPA published a booklet, *AOPA Congressional Relations Handbook*. The booklet was made available to all its members. In it, AOPA spells out how to influence legislation. It begins with the statement, "This handbook is a brief but, we trust, adequate and not too dull guide to the Federal legislative process, the most effective methods and techniques to influence it, and how and to whom their use should be addressed."

The booklet goes on to say, "It has become AOPA's responsibility to keep abreast of legislative matters affecting general aviation and to inform the members when necessary. The situation may call for concerted, aggressive action. . . ."

In explaining to its members why they have the right to influence their elected officials, AOPA wrote in the booklet, "Your Congressmen are politicians, in the best sense of the word. Politicians want to stay in office. They do this by getting reelected. But to get reelected, they must respond to the will of their constituents."

The booklet goes on to explain how to influence a senator or representative. It covers such practical matters as how to. address the member's elected official, what to say in person, and what to say in a letter. AOPA does not contribute as a group to any politician's campaign fund. But it encourages its members to do so. The booklet points out how expensive it is to run for office. And it says, "Your Congressional contacts will be even more effective if you lend some material support to your Congressman when he needs it." As defined in the booklet, material support can consist of money or time.

The rest of the booklet contains the names and hometowns of all United States representatives and senators, and a listing of the committees on which they serve.

The cost of producing and distributing this ninety-six page booklet, which includes liberal use of illustrations, was never reported as a lobbying expense by AOPA. When asked how AOPA justifies the exclusion of such projects from its quarterly financial reports to Congress, Robert Monroe replied, "Our legislative handbook is guidance and education rather than being for the promotion or defeat of a particular piece of legislation." Under the loophole of the lobbying act, Monroe and AOPA are quite right in their interpretation of what must be reported.

Monroe explained other aspects of AOPA's lobbying activities, lobbying in the accepted use of the term but perhaps not in the congressional definition under the act.

"We encourage our members to turn around and make their

thoughts known to their particular congressman. It seems to be working out pretty well. Besides the *Congressional Handbook* we publish, we also put out bulletins having to do with specific proposed rule making. We did this with the high-density issue. We also did it with the Airport Development Act, airport aid, customs overtime legislation, and so on. We encourage the members to write their congressmen. The member will generally send us a copy of his letter. And very often he'll send us a copy of the answer he receives from his congressman. Therefore we have a very rapid feedback and we can tell what individual congressional thought is, and we know what the individual congressman is saying and thinking, and we can personally approach that congressman. Or we can give the members more ammunition to go back to those congressmen and take another crack at them."

AOPA also makes good use of the lobbying act's exclusion of regulatory agencies from being under its intent and control. AOPA makes liberal use of its "insiders" within the FAA and conducts campaigns of influence over the Federal Aviation Administration. All this activity is exempt from lobbying controls, despite the fact that much of AOPA's search for influence over the FAA is conducted through senators and representatives. AOPA does many special mailings to its membership whenever the FAA proposes rule changes. One of these special mailings was made during the high-density summer of 1968, when the FAA was considering placing restrictions on the operations of private aviation at heavy traffic hubs. AOPA considered these proposals detrimental to all private aviation. The association issued a "Special Action Bulletin" calling members to action. The bulletin suggested the following:

"AOPA has warned that new restrictions to reduce air travel congestion and delay could cripple your flying. The FAA has now proposed such restrictions. This tells you what to do and what's involved. Time is limited. YOU SHOULD ACT NOW!

What to do:

1. Send two (2) copies of your comments on this proposal to
    Federal Aviation Administration
    Office of General Counsel
    Attn: Rules Docket GC-24
    800 Independence Avenue SW
    Washington, D.C. 20590

2. Send one (1) copy of your comments to both your Senators and your Representative with a letter or note asking them to use all their influence with the FAA in support of your position. Address them as follows:
    [Letter form spelled out]

3. Send AOPA a copy, Attn: V.J. Kayne

4. Follow up your letter to your Congressman with a personal or telephone contact if possible and emphasize your concern."

The bulletin went on to explain the issues at stake and instructed the members in what facts to use and positions to take.

None of this activity by AOPA comes under the lobbying legislation because it is the FAA, not the Congress, that is involved.

Is this kind of lobbying effective?

Extremely so.

The philosophy behind AOPA's thinking, and that of most other lobbying groups, is clear, sound, and basic. An elected official in Washington is, of occupational necessity, sensitive to those folks back home who, besides holding their votes as a token of appreciation for a friendly congressman, can contribute time and money to his next campaign for reelection to office. Private aircraft owners are, for the most part, members of the more affluent segment of any community. A survey by a news magazine showed that, of persons purchasing new aircraft for private use in 1963, the median income of the buyers was $33,300; 78 percent of the buyers were businessmen and 70 percent were in top management jobs. These private pilots and/or private aircraft owners are actively courted by politicians during an election period as a prime source of campaign funds. They also serve the vital function of providing swift and, most often, free air transportation for a politician as he attempts to visit outlying areas of his constituency. Then, too, it is the affluent member of a community who is more prone to make his voice heard in local matters.

There is also the avid involvement of the private pilot with his hobby. Congressman Richard Ottinger of New York indicated to me what the zeal of a constituent with a special interest means to an elected official.

"Any well-organized minority can cause quite a ripple," Ottinger said. "Take a look at the gun control people. They're a distinct minority of the American people, but they're highly organized and have a single purpose. I've been an advocate of strong gun control. The people in my district who are also for strong gun control have a diffuse interest. It's one of many interests they have. They'll be happy to vote against you on other issues even though they agree with you on gun control. The other people have a single purpose, and their principal interest in life is guns, and anyone who promotes gun legislation will find them going out and working against him. This is what you find with the aviation issue, also. Those who are concerned, the passengers, don't have very strong feelings about this one issue. They're interested in many things. But the private pilot—it's his hobby and love and principal interest. He's much more active in his pursuit of his interests. Private pilots, like gun buffs, make their voices heard far out of proportion to their numbers."

I asked Ottinger about AOPA and its programs to influence Congress and the FAA.

"As this aviation industry grows, there's going to be a terrible problem of airplanes just getting out of the way of each other. There will have to be order injected into the system. Like the law and order question today. You just don't have total freedom in an ordered society. People run into each other and there have to be some guidelines by which we must live with each other. But I've found AOPA to be quite unreasonable, as opposed to some of the local flying groups in my congressional district. I don't think AOPA advances its position or cause by being unreasonable. I think anyone who refuses to look at the problems as they really are and says that anything that touches me is no good—the hell with you—it's very hard to deal with that posture. It's hard to do what's right."

AOPA is well aware of its members' deep involvement with flying. Through constant prodding of its members, AOPA is confident of a steady stream of mail reaching the members of Congress and the decision makers of the FAA. When this mail reaches Congress and the FAA, the recipients of it can do little else but react favorably to the one-sided display on issues by the "folks back home."

Such crusades on the part of special interest groups are certainly within the established framework of Washington politics. In its purest state, lobbying can be beneficial to the nation. Each member of Congress finds himself pressed for time as a myriad of issues and problems competes for his attention. Obviously, no member of Congress can be expected to become expert in all things. Special interest groups are able to inform the legislator on the salient and meaningful aspects of the issue. But this pure and beneficial side of lobbying is seldom the case. Most often, lobbying is a concerted and directed effort at influence, one side in an issue pitted against another, each hoping to shape an elected official's thinking to his own particular viewpoint.

In the case of aviation, AOPA and ATA have emerged as the two most powerful combatants. As pointed out earlier, ATA speaks for the airlines as corporate entities, its arguments and conclusions weighed against the commercial interests of the airline industry. On the other hand, AOPA gallantly speaks for the "little guy," the individual threatened with extinction under the shadow of the multimillion-dollar airline industry. ATA is considered to have an ax to grind, a corporate, profit-honed ax. In contrast, AOPA speaks for *freedom*, a most cherished concept in our democracy. The battle lines have become that basic, as presented by the two sides in the argument—individual freedom versus corporate profit. AOPA enjoys this simplification of terms. ATA, try as it might, has difficulty in shaking its spokesman-for-large-industry status. Were ATA's efforts to be supplemented by an airline passenger association, the battle would take on a different dimension. It would then be 500,000 "little guys" versus 150 million "little guys"—airline passengers seeking their freedom of safe and efficient public air travel.

"There should be a vocal airline passenger group," New York Congressman Lester Wolff told me. "They are the ultimate victims, after all."

The airline passenger is seldom heard from. Members of Congress whom I interviewed agree, to a man, that it is rare to receive correspondence from airline passengers concerning air travel. The FAA hears even less from the airline passenger.

In the high-density issue of the summer of 1968, the FAA proposed rule changes that would alleviate, at least temporarily, the congestion at the major airports. Part of the suggested program of change was to limit the number of flights from each airport during peak hours. Under the proposed change in rules, both the airlines and private aviation would be given a set number of operational slots, the suggested number decreasing the frequency of operation for both groups at these airports. The FAA announced the proposed rule changes and waited for the comments to come in. As noted earlier, AOPA sent a "Special Action Bulletin" to its members urging them to write the FAA and Congress.

The total number of comments to reach the FAA on the high-density issue was 3,142.

Forty-three comments supported the rule changes. Most of these supported the changes in the hope that a reduction in the number of flights would alleviate the noise problem in their communities.

Two thousand ninety-nine were against the new rules. A member of the FAA's General Counsel's Office noted, "Replies were repetitious, and represented two principal classes of users of the airports concerned, the private small airplanes and large executive business aircraft. The former were represented primarily by the AOPA while the latter were represented by the NBAA. These comments, with a few exceptions, were opposed to the rule."

The FAA, reacting to private aviation's feelings on the proposed rule changes, attempted to kill the proposal within the agency. A few years ago, it would probably have succeeded in this attempt. But as an agency under the new Department of Transportation, the FAA had to answer to its new boss. The DOT responded by insisting that the proposed rule changes be implemented in some form.

AOPA was not the only industry segment unhappy with the proposed rule changes. The airlines also protested. With the increase in passenger and cargo demand for airline service, a cutback in operations from the large traffic hubs could only prove harmful, and would inhibit the growth of air travel deemed healthy by government and industry leaders. In a speech given to members of Sigma Delta Chi, the professional journalistic fraternity, in September, 1968, David Thomas, acting administrator of the FAA, said, "The proposed rule is a limiting, restrictive measure. And the suppression of air commerce is clearly not conducive to economic growth or long-range industry progress. . . . Restrictions, therefore, should be temporary."

Initially, the proposed rule changes called for Kennedy, LaGuardia, Newark, O'Hare, and Washington National airports to be allocated 80, 60, 60, 135, and 60 operations per hour respectively. These limitations were to be effective from 6 A.M. to midnight. In the case of Kennedy Airport, 70 of these hourly operations would be reserved for scheduled airlines, 5 for air taxis, and 5 for other operations, with the exception of the period from 5 P.M. to 8 P.M., when all 80 operational slots would be reserved for the airlines. The other airports named in the proposed rule changes did not have the all-airline restriction during any time periods. At LaGuardia, of the 60 hourly operations, 48 would go to the airlines, 6 to air taxis, and 6 to other operations. Newark would have 40 slots for airlines, 10 for air taxis, and 10 for other operations; O'Hare, 115 airline slots, 10 air taxis, and 10 other operations; Washington National, 40 slots for airlines, 8 for air taxis, and 12 for other operations.

In addition, the new rules would call for every aircraft under the restrictions to be capable of maintaining an airspeed of 150 knots while under the jurisdiction of air traffic approach control, to be equipped with a radar beacon transponder, a sophisticated radar device, and to be operated with two pilots in the cockpit.

All these new limitations were to be in effect only when weather was such that instrument flight rules prevailed. When weather permitted the use of visual flight rules, additional flights would be permitted over the hourly quotas.

The airlines opposed the rule changes but agreed to abide by them as a needed interim measure until the ATC system and airport capacity could be expanded to allow increased operations.

A surprising number of influential leaders in private aviation backed up the need for some sort of control and restriction in high-density areas. Robert B. Parke, in an editorial in *Flying*, a popular magazine for private pilots, said, "We believe that if there is to be any sanity in the system, the very few heavily congested areas should be restricted to IFR-equipped planes flown by IFR-rated pilots. Nor will we fight a restriction in these areas that calls for reasonable speed compatibility. Both Alan S. Boyd, Secretary, DOT, and Dave Thomas deserve all credit for subjecting themselves, in the interests of finding solutions to an intolerable situation, to the torment and tedium that resulted. If either man can be faulted, it must be on the grounds that they didn't act sooner. But at long last there is to be some movement, and we are not at all convinced that in the long haul general aviation will suffer."

An article in *The Pilot*, of October, 1968, was headlined, "DOT Capitulates to Airlines." In it, the private pilot association said, "AOPA intends to forcefully oppose this proposed rule making with every means at our command. . . ."

AOPA was forced to carry the banner into battle almost alone. By this time, other groups representing various segments of the private aviation industry had begun to disassociate themselves from AOPA's absolute stand on the high-density issue. At least one such association, the National Business Aircraft Association (NBAA), had begun to adopt this arm's-length position earlier than 1968. John Woods, assistant senior director of operations for NBAA, has very strong feelings about the need for civil aviation to pull together for the good of the industry. He refers to AOPA and ATA as the "high-pitched squeaks at both ends." NBAA feels it occupies a reasonable, middle-ground position in the battle, one destined to prevail. During my long interview with Woods, and in a thorough reading of NBAA policy and position papers, there is seldom found a statement that takes an absolute and vehement stand.

"We've been accused of being too statesmanlike by our members," Woods told me. "That's why our rebuttal to the high-density proposals by the FAA seems flamboyant, at least when compared to our stands over the past twenty-one years."

NBAA's relatively calm position is not to be mistaken for apathy or weakness. On the contrary, NBAA wages aggressive and continual programs in an attempt to put its corporate aviation story across to Congress and the FAA. NBAA's statesmanlike stance is both naturally acquired and strategically conceived. As an association representing many members with high stakes in the decisions to come, NBAA recognizes the diminishing effectiveness of shrill and unreasonable demands. The airlines are here to stay, and public needs will ultimately prevail. I asked Max Karant of AOPA why he thought associations such as NBAA have begun pulling away from AOPA's positions.

"AOPA is the American Automobile Association of the air," Karant answered. "NBAA is like the bus operators would be. By their very nature, these corporations that make up the membership of NBAA act very much like the airlines do. NBAA is the ATA of private aviation. They operate like airlines, they look like airlines, and they are like airlines. NBAA and AOPA have different goals. I have always had the unpleasant sensation of realizing that NBAA would probably settle for going into the Port Authority airports in New York while seeing us barred from those airports."

I asked Karant if NBAA saw the handwriting on the wall and wanted to go with a winner, the airlines.

"Maybe so," was Karant's reply.

A similar pulling away from AOPA's extreme positions was taken by the scheduled air taxi operators. As a group, they welcomed a CAB decision in September of 1968 that recognized the air taxi industry as an arm of commercial transportation and would thus bring it under the more stringent controls placed upon the airlines. Until the CAB decision, air taxis had been considered just another part of private aviation and had found themselves represented in certain matters by such spokesmen as AOPA. Controls were minimal over air taxi operations, despite the fact that they carried over five million paying passengers in 1968. The accident statistics for the air taxi industry were appalling, and becoming worse with each year. The new restrictions placed on air taxi operators would prove costly and difficult. Still, the air taxi industry heartily adopted the CAB recommendations and is at work bringing itself up to standard.

All this has left AOPA pretty much alone in championing private aviation's traditional cries for total freedom to all airspace, handling on a first-come, first-served basis, and exemption from any further government regulation. This lonely position has not dimmed the vigor and optimism with which AOPA attacks its given task. During the high-density proposals by the FAA, AOPA ran a series of advertisements in leading newspapers around the country. In these ads, AOPA claimed that more people were transported on private aviation aircraft than on commercial airlines. It based its claim on an FAA study.

"The Federal Aviation Administration, in an official report, stated that the number of people served by general aviation approximates the number carried as passengers by all the domestic carriers. Thus, one half of the public which uses air transportation use their own planes for the same reasons you use your automobile." The ads were headlined, "SHOULD THE AIRLINES BE ALLOWED TO TELL EVERY SECOND PERSON THAT THEY CAN'T TRAVEL BY AIR?"

What AOPA didn't tell the readers of these ads was that the FAA study to which they referred had been conducted in 1965 at a selected number of FAA control towers and flight service stations, at which private aviation pilots would file flight plans. The FAA decided that only one in five private aviation flights had a flight plan filed in conjunction with its operation. The FAA further decided that the average load factor in each private aviation aircraft was 3.1 persons. By applying these sets of "let's suppose" figures, the FAA came up with numbers indicating that, in 1965, private aviation aircraft carried roughly half as many people as the airlines did. AOPA then added what it claimed were the number of local private aviation operations in any given year—those flights that depart and arrive at the same airport, including much student flying and similar activity—and came up with a figure to support the claims in its ads.

I asked Robert Monroe, AOPA's congressional liaison man, about the ads, and whether it was prudent of AOPA to base advertisements on such shaky statistical material. He answered first by blaming the government for not gathering better statistics on private aviation activity on which such organizations as AOPA could hang their hats in the aviation confrontation. He concluded by saying, "I'm inclined to say that it isn't as good evidence as we would like to have, but it's the best evidence available. In the kind of scrap we're in, you use all the weapons you have at your disposal and command for survival, and this is essentially a survival exercise."

AOPA stepped up its campaign against the FAA's proposed rule changes. To the surprise of a number of industry people, secure in the thought that the situation had become so bad at the hub areas that the public air transportation position had to prevail, the FAA retreated under AOPA's pressure and tried to substitute another rule for the one restricting operations at high-density airports. The substitute rule dealt with flow control. Under this rule, whenever delays forecast for aircraft flying into New York under instrument flight rules (IFR) exceeded one hour, aircraft would be held on the ground at their departure airports, rather than in holding patterns while airborne. The DOT quickly flexed its supervisory muscle over the FAA. It not only went ahead with the previous proposed rules, but adopted the substitute rule as well.

Undaunted, AOPA continued the fight. And it managed to bring about significant modifications in the proposed rule changes which went into effect on June 1, 1969. The major change involved the 5 P.M. to 8 P.M. time segment at Kennedy Airport. In the revised version of the rule changes, that three-hour period would not be restricted to airline operations only. In addition, the proposed requirements for two pilots, transponder equipment, and speed minimums were dropped.

This kind of success by AOPA is indicative of the association's influence over the FAA. More important, when the rule changes are viewed from an overall vantage point, the success of AOPA becomes even greater. Because of the FAA's decision to make room for private planes at the busy, large hub airports, fewer airline schedules could be accommodated. The result? Less service for the airline passenger, growing in number but diminishing in the consideration shown him.

AOPA's success in the high-density issue did not result from a sudden spurt of activity by the association. AOPA's efforts in the high-density question were offered as part of its continuing program of attempts to influence the FAA and Congress. Certain of these efforts are worthwhile and beneficial to the aviation community. The AOPA Foundation, a nonprofit organization dedicated to air safety, has engaged in numerous projects designed to foster better airmanship. Currently, the foundation is working closely with the FAA in a program to revalidate flight instructors every two years. The foundation, and AOPA itself, conducts refresher clinics around the country in which private pilots may brush up on rusty skills and acquire necessary new skills demanded by the advancing state of the aviation art. In its magazine *The Pilot*, AOPA constantly urges its members to follow safety suggestions offered by AOPA, encourages them to file flight plans, abstain from drinking prior to flight, upgrade their flying skills with periodic instruction, become familiar with weather patterns and check weather before conducting any flight, and observe other basic safety procedures deemed proper for the safe conduct of flight. Of course, such joint ventures as the instructor revalidation program, in which AOPA and the FAA join forces, generate substantial benefit to AOPA in its relationship with the FAA. Ties are tightened, relationships are solidified, and understanding grows, all to be possibly brought into play at some future, controversial time. Still, the industry benefits.

Despite the concern for safety demonstrated by AOPA and especially by Max Karant, the association stands solidly against any changes in regulation offered by the FAA in the pursuit of increased air safety. In each area of safety mentioned above, AOPA has worked against regulation or legislation that would make such safety procedures mandatory. In certain cases, it has ventured into such vehement and distasteful proclamations as to bring strong rebuttal from its own membership. In the hassle over private pilot recertification, AOPA used its monthly *Confidential Newsletter*, distributed only to members, to attack ATA's call for periodic retraining and retesting of private pilots to assure they maintained an acceptable level of competence. AOPA said the following in its newsletter of November, 1967:

"AOPA comment: a level of competence, perhaps, like that demonstrated by the airlines over the Grand Canyon (128 dead), over Staten Island (134 dead), the TWA-Eastern collision north of N.Y., the landing of the TWA 707 at Ohio State University's airport, the TWA DC-9 that ran down the general aviation twin (26 dead) near Urbana, O., the United 727 that landed so hard at Salt Lake City it burned and killed 42, the American 727 that hit a hill near Cincinnati and killed 58, and so on and on?"

The above and other statements have eroded AOPA's

image to some extent. Still, it remains as a potent and influential force in the aviation industry, and particularly in the halls of Congress.

During the high-density issue of 1968, ninety-four individual congressmen offered written comments to the FAA concerning the proposed rule changes. Forty-five of these congressmen used correspondence from constituents as the basis for their involvement in the issue (there were 650 pieces of correspondence from citizens to members of Congress). The remaining forty-nine congressmen issued personal comments on the proposed rule changes. Eight of these favored the proposal, four because it might alleviate noise in their districts. Thirty-eight of the forty-one congressmen against the proposed changes cited the same reasons as those given by AOPA for being against adoption of the new rules.

Of all comments received by the FAA on the high-density issue, those from members of Congress were weighted the heaviest. The FAA, like all other federal regulatory agencies, depends upon Congress for its very existence. Congress, through the appropriate committees, must allocate funds to the agency for year-to-year operations. It is perfectly understandable that the staff at the FAA should listen closely to what members of Congress say. It is equally understandable that AOPA, aware of the FAA's dependence upon Congress, should spend a great deal of time wooing congressmen to private aviation's way of thinking. The 150,000 members of AOPA are the primary vehicle through which AOPA can tell its story to Congress. And there are other ways, not initiated by AOPA or any other group representing private aviation interests, but conveniently part of the activities of members of the House and Senate.

The Congressional Flying Club is very much like any other flying club in the country. Members pay dues and utilize aircraft owned or leased by the club for the members' enjoyment. Perhaps the most significant difference between this club and others is that members of the Congressional Flying Club are also members of the Congress of the United States.

Donald Clausen, Republican representative from California's First Congressional District, has been the club's most enthusiastic member. Affairs of the club are administrated through Congressman Clausen's offices in Washington.

The club utilizes two Piper Cherokee aircraft. It will also soon begin treating its members to training in a General Aviation Trainer (GAT-1), a new ground simulator manufactured by the Link Division of the General Precision Corporation. Congressman Clausen gave the dedication speech at the 1967 unveiling of the GAT-1 in New York, and has been a frequent booster of the trainer. The GAT-1 to be put into operation for members of the Congressional Flying Club and, according to Clausen, for all members of Congress who are willing for this exposure to private aviation was donated by General Precision. Its cost to those who *must pay* for this equipment with all options runs about $14,000.

It was this writer's feeling while researching this book in Washington that senators and representatives had far greater access to indoctrination by private aviation than to that by the scheduled airlines. There are currently over fifteen members of the House or Senate enrolled as active members in the Congressional Flying Club. Many others are exposed through attendance at meetings in a nonmember role. Now, with such a sophisticated piece of training equipment housed almost in the very halls of Congress, exposure will become even greater.

I asked Congressman Clausen about this exposure and whether it didn't present a one-sided case to the congressmen, especially in view of the decisions they must make regarding all aviation.

"I don't think so," he answered. "What we're trying to do in the Congressional Flying Club is give as many members of Congress [as possible] some education and exposure to aviation in general, not just from general aviation's side of things." Clausen's stated goal is honorable. Whether the activities of the Congressional Flying Club and the presence of the GAT-1 general aviation trainer do anything to further the goal of overall understanding of aviation remains a debatable issue.

I asked Jack Shea, a sales promotion executive of General Precision, why the firm had donated the GAT-1 to the Congressional Flying Club.

"It's a loan, I guess," Shea said, "to give them something to use for a while to give the pilots in the Congressional Flying Club a chance to get their instrument skills brushed up."

"Doesn't it also present private aviation's side of things to the congressmen?" I asked.

"Well, as I understand it from the Congressional Flying Club, the GAT is to be used for education for those congressmen who maybe don't always vote along logical lines in aviation matters."

I asked Shea whether AOPA was cooperating with General Precision in placing the GAT-1 in Congress.

"No, I don't think so. Of course, I'm sure they're pleased with it. AOPA says it's looking for understanding and I guess they'd be in favor of seeing the GAT-1 in Congress."

AOPA does involve itself in the Congressional Flying Club whenever possible. Robert Monroe, AOPA's Congressional liaison man, told me, "I'm an auxilary member of the Congressional Flying Club. All this means is I pay twenty-five dollars to the club. It's not a very active club and doesn't do very much."

I mentioned the GAT-1 trainer.

"Somebody's helping out," Monroe commented. "That may do us some good. It would be to our advantage to see the Congressional Flying Club strong, and we would give them as much help as they wanted. We've worked with them on a number of occasions when they've taken tours. We've conned somebody into bringing in an airplane so the members would have something to fly around and ride on. We also provided chart material. The fellow who helped start the club was never very favorably disposed to AOPA. He used to work for the FAA and then became a rep here in Washington for one of the manufacturers. He's doing consulting work now."

The Congressional Flying Club currently has about fifty members. Ground schools are conducted on a regular basis with volunteers from the FAA and nearby flight schools. Congressman Clausen estimates the lease cost of the two Piper Cherokees at about six hundred dollars per month, the members' dues and fees for the use of the planes generating this monthly money. I asked Clausen for a list of members of the club. He refused my request.

There are other means by which members of Congress are exposed to the private aviation line of thinking. One obvious way is through membership in AOPA. According to Monroe, AOPA has two senators and fifteen representatives on the membership rolls. *The Pilot* regularly tips its association hat to these members by featuring them in articles. Monroe refused me a list of congressional members, but a scanning of *The Pilot* gives some indication of who they are. Some of these members, and their AOPA Membership numbers, are: Morris K. Udall (AOPA 95586) of Arizona; Donald R. Clausen (AOPA 84366) of California; Senator Peter Dominick (AOPA 176549) of Colorado; Hastings Keith (AOPA 205712) of Massachusetts; William E. Minshall (AOPA 93939) of Ohio and John W. Davis (AOPA 243284).

In addition, AOPA makes reference to "friends" in Congress, such as James T. Broyhill of North Carolina, Senator Howard Cannon of Nevada, Senator Gordon Allott of Colorado, Richard Ichord of Missouri, Donald Rumsfeld of Illinois, and Robert T. Stafford of Vermont. AOPA helps its members understand which members of Congress are potential allies by placing an asterisk next to their names in the

Congressional Relations Handbook to indicate that those so designated are active private aviators.

Of all congressional friends of private aviation, Congressman Don Clausen is the most active and vocal. An eloquent and able legislator, Clausen manages to include favorable references to private aviation in virtually every congressional debate in which he participates. Long and convincing testimony to the values of private aviation comes up in debates on education, communism, poverty, juvenile delinquency, and religion. Clausen deeply believes in private aviation. A pilot with some fifteen thousand hours of flight time and the former owner of aviation charter services in California, he has indicated on many occasions his belief in the power of aviation. In a message to AOPA on its twenty-fifth anniversary, which was printed in full in *The Pilot* under the headline, "Birthday Messages from Members and friends," he said, "I submit again that expanded use of aircraft can be one of our most efficient and effective weapons to win the cold war." He congratulated AOPA on its twenty-five years of "great service and leadership." He went on to say, "As we look to the next 25 years of progress, I believe it will become increasingly necessary for the general aviation community to express itself more boldly." Private aviation has not disappointed its leading congressional member.

I asked Robert Monroe about AOPA's association with Congressman Clausen.

"It's probably not as close as he [Clausen] would like it to be," Monroe responded. "Congressmen, after all, in a relationship with people like us, are fairly demanding. We've given Clausen what we consider to be a fair amount of treatment in *The Pilot*. He would like a lot more. A congressman is always looking for publicity."

Congressman Fletcher Thompson of Georgia, a relatively new member of Congress, is also an avid booster of private aviation. Athletic and charming (he insisted I have Georgia

peanuts and Coke bottled in Atlanta during the interview),
Congressman Thompson advocates some moderation of the
positions taken by both ATA and AOPA. A member of
AOPA (AOPA 187826) and an experienced private pilot
with commercial and multiengine ratings, Congressman
Thompson called for increased controls over private aviation
following the Hendersonville, North Carolina, midair accident. His position was quoted in the July 22, 1968, issue of
the *Atlanta Journal*. Thompson felt his remarks had been misinterpreted by his friends in private aviation, and *The Pilot*
invited him to explain his position in an article. He did so,
assuring the private aviation community he was still a friend,
but at the same time standing on some of the changes he had
called for earlier.

There is another vehicle through which members of Congress
receive indoctrination on private aviation's problems and
operations. This is the Civil Air Patrol.

The Civil Air Patrol (CAP) dates back to 1941 when, as
the nation was faced with another world war, leaders in government began debating to what use civilian air power could be
put in national defense. The CAP was formed; its volunteer
civilian members engaged in such noncombat missions as trans-
porting needed military parts, patrolling power lines in
search of saboteurs, searching for missing aircraft, patrolling
forests, and providing courier service for the Army Air Force
and other military organizations. Soon the members of CAP
began venturing into more combative and dangerous missions.
They flew reconnaissance missions over coastal waters in
search of enemy submarines. They even began dropping depth
charges from their light planes, the explosives slung under
the wings in makeshift holders. The towing of airborne targets for antiaircraft gun practice was another hazardous
mission for the CAP; twenty-three airplanes were destroyed
and seven CAP members killed in this activity.

Today, the CAP boasts over 85,000 adult and cadet members, over 38,000 senior members, and over 47,000 cadet

members, ages thirteen through twenty-one. The primary mission of the CAP today is search and rescue. Nearly three-fourths of all flying hours expended on S&R missions in 1967 were flown by CAP members and their airplanes. These members flew 20,909 hours searching for downed aircraft. One hundred nineteen persons were saved and 1,342 persons were assisted through the S&R program.

One of the advantages of the CAP is that a cadet member can learn to fly and even receive his FAA private pilot's license through the CAP. There is good reason for the Air Force to continue to provide assistance, both monetary and administrative, to the CAP program. One of the stated purposes of the CAP is to make the nation aware of aviation and its contribution to our society. Many cadets, trained in flight through their CAP affiliation, go on to be Air Force pilots. Thus, the CAP is a valuable recruiting tool for the Air Force.

All this CAP history and activity had little to do with the Congress until a charter was issued to establish a Congressional Squadron of the CAP. Commanded by Congressman Lester Wolff of New York, the Congressional CAP Squadron has become an active organization in Washington since its inception in December, 1967.

Each member of Congress received a letter early in 1968 from Congressman Wolff and Congressman Jerry Pettis, the new squadron's executive officer, inviting him and his family to join the Congressional CAP. Senators were promised the rank of lieutenant colonel, the same rank each would receive from the Air Force Reserve. The letter referred to such activities as pilot upgrading courses, learn-to-fly clinics, and FAA indoctrination. AOPA mentioned the new squadron in the April, 1968, issue of *The Pilot* and noted that Congressman Wolff expected to enroll members of the Congressional Flying Club in his squadron. The membership drive was an obvious success; by the summer of 1968, twenty-three members of Congress had joined.

It is not this writer's purpose to malign the CAP by including it in those organizations that influence Congress toward the private aviation position. On the contrary, the CAP has proved itself to be a most valuable and worthwhile national resource. But its new presence in Congress does serve, inadvertently, to further the cause of private aviation. The stress is placed upon private flying for its members.

And so on.

Corporations often provide corporate aircraft for the swift and personal transportation of members of Congress.

The NBAA lobbies Congress.

The National Utility Airplane Council (representing light plane manufacturers) lobbies Congress.

The Flying Lawyers lobby Congress.

All sorts of private aviation groups and individuals lobby Congress, and the FAA. One, the Gates Aviation Corporation, testified during the high-density hearings of 1968 and pleaded the cause of private aviation. One of its main points was summed up by an FAA legal counsel in his report of the hearings. The Gates spokesman told the committee that business jets fly the greatest brains, not the greatest number of persons. He asked that a value be placed upon this fact.

The airline passenger, perhaps less intelligent than the business jet passenger, according to the Gates theory, but certainly of some importance, is silent. His only hope in the aviation dilemma is that ATA can present an effective case for the airline position. Based upon past performance, the image of the big industry profit makers has hindered ATA's effectiveness considerably. The "little guy"—the private pilot—has emerged victorious in most of the individual battles. This fact is surely a tribute to the various organizations that speak on behalf of private aviation, AOPA leading the way.

"I do bookkeeping on members of Congress," Robert Monroe of AOPA told me. "I do this and report their activities in our magazine. We want our people to know those who are doing something for us and those who are not."

In lobbying circles, it's called doing your homework and AOPA does its homework well. Drew Pearson and Jack Anderson wrote in their "Washington Merry-Go-Round" column of September 3, 1968, "Probably the biggest problem Secretary of Transportation Alan Boyd has to cope with is the powerful lobby of the private airplanes. This lobby, the AOPA, the Aircraft Owners and Pilots Association, is the equivalent of the National Rifle Association in its influence over Congress. Its theory is that one executive in a private plane is more important than 180 tourists in a big jet 707."

Pearson and Anderson went on to say, "When it comes to building more airports or even improving the traffic regulations at existing airports, the Congress bows to the powerful AOPA lobby. And Congress runs for cover whenever anyone tries to put commercial traffic ahead of private traffic."

The high-density issue of 1968 is only the most recent case in which private aviation proved its might in dealing with Congress and the FAA. There have been many issues in the past, one of which dealt with the right of the private pilot to drink before and even during the operation of his aircraft. Before the controversy over the drinking-flying problem, the private pilot was free to do just that—drink and fly.

He still is.

CHAPTER FIVE

The Right to Drink and Fly

In December, 1966, the nation's press reported on an FAA study, released late that year, which related alcohol consumption to fatal private aviation accidents. United Press International released the story on its national newswire, thereby doing all of aviation a disservice. UPI meant well. The FAA study indicated that 30 percent of all fatal private aviation accidents *involved* pilots whose blood alcohol levels were above those deemed to impair judgment and coordination. UPI reported that the FAA study found 30 percent of private aviation accidents had been *caused* by drinking pilots.

Private aviation jumped on UPI's error and used it to claim that the FAA report was erroneous in its conclusions. With AOPA leading the way, private aviation pointed to UPI as but another example of forces out to crush aviation's little guys. Unfortunately, the true meaning of the FAA study was buried beneath the avalanche of protest. In fact the study showed *beyond doubt* that private pilots drank and flew in too many cases.

AOPA titled an editorial in the March, 1967, issue of *The Pilot*, "Us Drunks." In it, AOPA dwelt on UPI's misinterpretation of the study's findings. The FAA was taken to task because, under a strict reading of the agency's mission, it is not empowered to determine causal factors in fatal aviation accidents. That job is given to the National Transportation Safety Board. The editorial concluded, "No pilot with good judgment and a reasonable amount of common sense will fly during or immediately after drinking. The few who do should be reported to the authorities by any pilot who sees it happening, both to save the life of the fool involved and to prevent any further blackening of the good name of general aviation." Good advice. AOPA, and every other informed voice in aviation, is against drinking and flying. But the suggestion in the editorial to report a drinking pilot to the proper authority would be nothing more than an academic exercise in futility. *There is no law, rule, or regulation prohibiting a pilot from drinking, either before he flies or even during flight.*

The FAA study on alcohol-related private aviation accidents was conducted by Dr. Stanley Mohler, chief of the Aeromedical Applications Division of the FAA. Dr. Mohler is also a member of long standing of AOPA. Needless to say, his study and its subsequent release to the public did not endear him to his fellow AOPA members.

"There are many people in general aviation who hate my guts," he told me in his office in Washington.

But there were some who, even though private pilots themselves and members of AOPA, agreed with the intent and importance of Dr. Mohler's work. One, Kenneth H. Andrus (AOPA Member No. 175634), wrote a letter to *The Pilot.* He referred to the January, 1968, issue of the AOPA *Confidential Newsletter,* a monthly newsletter distributed to members only. Andrus wrote, "Again, in the January *Newsletter,* AOPA is defending pilots, and the statistics involved, concerning drinking and flying. Why should we try to downgrade and avoid the issue? Automobile safety legislators are already making themselves look silly in this same matter. . . . So the statistics in question are misleading and misinterpreted. This is true of almost all statistics ever compiled on any subject under Heaven. . . . Why are we trying to sweep this thing under the rug? Instead, why don't we work on this in the same manner the AOPA Safety Foundation has tackled other safety problems? An apparent fact to all of us is that far too many general aviation pilots are mixing drinking and flying."

AOPA did not agree with Andrus. It set about to attack the alcohol study from every possible angle, including a charge that Dr. Mohler had "loaded the deck" against private aviation by including in the 30 percent pilots whose luggage was found to have contained a bottle of whiskey, even though the man's blood alcohol level was negative. The major thrust, however, of AOPA's defense was that the blood alcohol level used by Dr. Mohler to indicate intoxication was too low. AOPA insisted that a reading of 15 mg%, the level used by Dr. Mohler to indicate impairment, was too low. AOPA pointed to other studies, dealing with drinking and driving, which used higher blood alcohol levels as indicators of impaired judgment and coordination.

Dr. Mohler's alcohol study was conducted over a four-year period. It started in 1963 with a modest 20 percent of fatal private aviation accidents given autopsy and toxicological investigation and analysis. The percentage tested increased until, by 1967, 74 percent of all fatal private aviation accidents were investigated for blood alcohol levels. This testing program was discharged primarily through the seven FAA regions, which in turn coordinated the work with approximately six thousand designated aviation medical examiners.

It is generally accepted by the medical community that one bottle of beer or one highball consumed by an average 150-pound man will produce a blood alcohol level reading of 15 mg%. This is also the amount of alcohol that the human body can rid itself of per hour. The use of milligrams percent (mg%) is the accepted measure of blood alcohol in clinical studies. It was Dr. Mohler's contention that the introduction of 15 mg% of alcohol into the human body would, in various degrees, affect the body's performance. There have been other studies in which a higher mg% level was used to denote influence of alcohol on the body, most of these dealing with the need for legal definition in cases of drivers suspected of being drunk. But other medical men in the aviation field tend to concur with the 15 mg% level as being the point at which an airman's efficiency begins to be affected. The increased skills and judgment needed to operate an aircraft, as opposed to driving a car, would in themselves necessitate the use of a lower mg% level.

Simply broken down, Dr. Mohler's study revealed the following:

	1963	1964	1965	1966	1967*
Total fatalities	900	980	1020	1123	1228
Number of fatalities tested for blood alcohol level	136	215	293	347	375
Percentage of those tested having positive levels	43%	39%	36%	27%	24%

* The 1967 figures were not included in the report issued to the press by the FAA.

Of those tested showing positive blood alcohol levels, the following were the percentages of the tested group falling into the listed milligram percentage (mg%) brackets:

	1963	1964	1965	1966	1967
Less than 50 mg%	32%	28%	43%	47%	47%
50–99 mg%	21	22	19	19	12
100–149 mg%	15	27	15	17	18
More than 150 mg%	32	23	23	17	23

AOPA used *The Pilot* to present its arguments against the alcohol study. It ran a two-part article written by Duane E. Best, a veteran private pilot, airline engineer-pilot, and freelance writer.

Part one of the article, published in the May, 1967, issue, devoted itself to questioning the mg% level used by Dr. Mohler. Various studies were cited, each favorable to AOPA's contention that a blood alcohol level of 15% was not sufficient to constitute intoxication of the pilot. These studies quoted by AOPA and Best were all related to highway programs in individual states. A survey of auto fatalities conducted by the Indiana University Department of Police Administration was quoted, in which the department concluded that blood alcohol levels over 40 mg% were "definitely associated with increased accident involvement." A study by the police department of Grand Rapids, Michigan, made the point that each individual's height, weight, and related physical characteristics played a part in the effect a given amount of alcohol would have on his ability to perform.

Best also devoted a substantial portion of the first part of his article to the inherent weaknesses in those tests used to determine blood alcohol levels.

All of the above material has validity within the framework of its intent and usefulness. But, unfortunately, the use of the material as a *defense* against Dr. Mohler's report falls far short on two important counts. One is the obvious fact that flying an airplane requires much more skill, judgment, and coordination than driving an automobile. An mg% level that would serve as legal evidence of drunkenness while driving has absolutely no relation to the mg% level that would hinder the performance of a pilot. Then, too, the effects of alcohol in the body increase with altitude; driver studies fail to have relevance to pilot studies for this reason, also.

Best also attacked the FAA's and Dr. Mohler's contention that alcohol played a part in a significant number of private aviation accidents. AOPA, and Best, turned to former CAB findings in which far fewer accidents listed alcohol as a causal factor. I asked Dr. Mohler about this during an interview in his Washington office.

"The policy of NTSB (and the CAB before that) was to use

50 mg% as a cutoff point. That's four average martinis. Anything below that would cause the NTSB to automatically drop alcohol as a causative factor. We maintain from our research that even one drink affects the judgment and behavior of an individual and can lead him to do dangerous acts that could lead to an accident. This is why the NTSB and its predecessor, the CAB, always came up with about half the alcohol-related findings we came up with in accidents. We didn't use the cutoff of four martinis. We start with one."

There is good reason for the CAB and NTSB to be conservative in their determinations of alcohol as a causative factor in airplane accidents. As the official agencies charged with determining cause, they have much at stake when the findings are released. The legal ramifications alone dictate caution in assigning blame that would, at once, introduce negligence into the picture.

Major William H. Berner, a physician in the U.S. Army attached to the CAB's Human Factors Section, commented, "When the CAB puts a pronouncement on an accident as to probable cause, this is different from just keeping statistics for edification so we are probably much more conservative [than the FAA]."

AOPA, in its foreword to Best's article, made much of its determination to gather all the facts and not whitewash the picture in the interests of its members and readers. If the reader of Best's two-part article accepts this claim of objectivity, he can then only surmise that Dr. Mohler and the FAA were 100 percent wrong in their findings and, even worse, deliberately stacked the deck against private aviation. Best goes as far in the article as to intimate that Dr. Mohler included case histories in which no clinical tests were conducted. Best claimed that witness reports and the finding of a broken liquor bottle near the scene of one accident were enough to include that case in the category of drinking pilot.

"That's absolutely untrue," Dr. Mohler told me when questioned about the charge made in the AOPA article. "We reported only biochemical determinations."

Clearly, AOPA's articles by Best were not published in the interest of "finding the facts and not whitewashing private aviation." Even Max Karant, who presumably hired Best and directed his efforts, has termed the article a "rebuttal." He has not done this publicly, however. The truth is that Best, under AOPA's direction, wrote a highly professional article that is no more unbiased than is this book. Both have a point of view.

There are other studies to which Duane Best might have referred in the drinking-flying controversy. A study conducted by Dr. Herman Heise concluded that individuals tested for judgment and sensory and motor functions, prior to and shortly after the consumption of alcohol, showed deterioration after consuming as little as two bottles of beer.

Dr. Ross A. McFarland wrote in his book, *Human Factors in Air Transportation*, that alcohol, even in small amounts, produces such aftereffects as:

1. A dulling of critical judgment.
2. A decreased sense of responsibility.
3. Diminished skill reactions and coordination.
4. Decreased speed and strength of muscular reflexes (even after one ounce of alcohol).
5. Twenty percent decrease in efficiency of eye movements during reading (after one ounce of alcohol).
6. Significantly increased frequency of errors (after one ounce of alcohol).
7. Constriction of visual fields.
8. Decreased ability to see under dim illumination.
9. Loss of efficiency of sense of touch.
10. Decrease of memory and reasoning ability.
11. Increased susceptibility to fatigue and decreased attention span.
12. Increased self-confidence with decreased insight into immediate capabilities and mental and physical status.

Dr. Mohler's study and resulting report concluded three major points:

1. One ounce of whiskey or one bottle of beer ingested during the period that immediately precedes flight planning prior to undertaking a flight can cause a significant impairment in airmanship.

2. Present evidence indicates that about one-third of the fatal accidents now being experienced in civil light aircraft today are facilitated directly or indirectly by ethyl alcohol ingestion.

3. Within the context of the report, an aggressive education program for general aviation airmen is indicated, and a substantial reduction may be accomplished in the incidence of light aircraft accidents.

Dr. Mohler's call for expanded education in this area for private pilots came only after a regulation was written and considered at the FAA that would have banned drinking eight hours prior to taking control of an airplane. This proposed regulation was dropped somewhere along the administrative way at the agency. AOPA was, of course, against the regulation. And it again made effective use of its voice in protesting this latest attempt to restrict the private pilot.

When I asked Dr. Mohler why the proposed drinking regulation had been defeated in the FAA, he replied, "We proposed an eight-hour gap from bottle to throttle. It went pretty high here [the FAA] before it was killed. It was killed because the airlines have a twenty-four hour rule and this would look like the FAA condoned a watered-down version. We obviously couldn't go to a twenty-four hour rule for light plane pilots. We couldn't because so many business and private pilots drink at the fly-in conventions (AOPA holds an annual fly-in for members at which clinics are held, meetings are conducted, and parties are thrown). You'll find quite a bit of alcohol consumed at these parties. And a lot of the people will be comsuming it on the last day of the meeting. These people can't be expected to sit around and dry out for an extra day. If you drink until the last evening and then go to bed, you'll be okay in the morning provided you haven't drunk to excess and have consumed a good quality whiskey."

QUESTION: Do you really think 150 million airline passengers should be concerned about a handful of affluent private pilots having their rights to an extra day of drinking?

MOHLER: (*Laughing*) Don't get me wrong. I personally was in favor of the rule. After it was all weighed, it was decided that it was a matter of individual discretion. And education.

QUESTION: But again, should airline passengers have to depend on this kind of discretion? It seems your study shows that discretion is lacking in a great many cases.

MOHLER: Probably not. That's why I was in favor of the rule to replace the existing one. We have 130 million airline passengers this year [1967] and they must be protected from a midair collision with some boozed-up light plane pilot.

Still, the old rule remains in force. It's of interest to note that the FAA has its own rule for its employees who pilot FAA aircraft. These employees are prohibited from drinking eight hours prior to flying. A similar do-as-I-say-not-as-I-do situation in the FAA exists with periodic retraining of private pilots. Although the agency does not require private pilots to upgrade themselves, it does require precisely this of its flying employees.

Part two of Duane Best's article made much of Dr. Mohler's claim that flying an airplane demanded greater attention and proficiency than driving an automobile. AOPA questioned this claim. The association wanted proof.

The following is a quote from Dr. Mohler's report on his study. It was written under the heading *Analysis of the Flying Task.*

"There are certain key factors in piloting a light aircraft. These include roll, pitch and yaw movements. There are such matters as 'velocity never exceed,' stalling speeds, drift movements, gusts and critical attitudes. The automobile presents an extremely simplified control picture with respect to the above points. [As a matter of fact, under most driving conditions, the automobile has none of these considerations.]

"In addition, the light plane pilot must navigate, must make appropriate control settings, must coordinate, and must make critical adjustments of the power, trim, mixture, propeller, etc., prior to take-off, during climb, en route, during descent, and when landing. He must exercise proper judgments concerning 'go' or 'no go' in different situations, a matter seriously compromised by the effects of alcohol on the cerebrum and on the emotional mechanisms.

"The pilot must operate the aircraft in the air at speeds many times those used by cars. When he changes the position of one control, almost certainly all the other controls will be affected. Weather factors in flying are far more critical than is the case for autos, and pilots must also calculate how the barometric pressure and the air temperature will influence his plane's lifting capabilities at given airfield lengths and with given weight loadings.

"Visibility factors concerned with haze, dust, rain or darkness, icing problems, and with the occurrence of the unanticipated (head winds, fuel shortage, engine or radio malfunction, etc.) must be dealt with quickly, correctly and skillfully. The leeway concering these factors for the automobile driver, as compared to the airplane pilot, is great. In addition, automobiles have yet to become involved in airport and en route radio procedures.

"Owners' handbooks for typical light single-engine and four-place retractable gear aircraft show 20 different pre-flight categories of items to check out, 5 specific starting maneuvers, 10 ground check operations, 10 pre-take-off checks, 7 climb operations, 10 categories of en route operations, 7 pre-landing operations, 3 landing operations and 8 shut-down items, all of which must be individually ascertained to ensure a successful flight accomplished with a reasonable level of safety. This makes an interesting comparison with the 10 items listed in current automobile owners' manuals.

"Obviously, flying as described above is considerably more complicated than driving, and offers eight times or more the opportunity for error than is the case with driving."

AOPA and Best refuted Dr. Mohler's claims. The manufacturers of light planes had conducted highly effective and energetic campaigns in the past to convince the population that flying was at least as easy as driving a car. National advertisements talked of the ease of flying—like taking a Sunday spin in the family buggy. These campaigns have been dropped, the criticism of them sufficient to bring about their demise. The claims made in the ads were simply too illogical. As a pilot and driver, I will add what assurance can be added to Dr. Mohler's position that driving *is* much easier than flying. True, advances in the design of light planes have made the act of simple piloting a less demanding one. But no design advances can lower the demands of piloting to anywhere near those of driving an automobile. To claim otherwise is either sincere ignorance or a calculated distortion of the facts.

A year after Best wrote his article for AOPA, he wrote a letter to *Flying*, another popular private aviation magazine. In his letter, Best said, "With the booming growth of our pilot population, I think it is absolutely necessary to keep reminding ourselves of the hazards inherent in drinking alcoholic beverages and piloting aircraft." One can't help wondering how convinced Best was in the first instance when he undertook to write the two-part article for AOPA.

Perhaps the most frustrating aspect of this whole question is that everyone in aviation preaches against mixing alcoholic beverages with piloting. AOPA has been an acknowledged leader in fostering improved safety in private aviation, and has issued frequent and stern warnings against drinking and flying. The NTSB is fully aware of the dangers of flying and drinking and says so at every turn. And the FAA issues educational bulletins warning of the ill effects alcohol has on airmen.

But no one will endorse a regulation *prohibiting* drinking before piloting an aircraft. No one except the airlines.

The most frequent defense used by the FAA and NTSB when questioned about a drinking-flying regulation is that a rule is already on the books of the FAA. The rule to which they refer is the one stating that a pilot will not operate an aircraft while under the influence of alcohol or drugs. It is, at best, an after-the-fact rule.

In preparing his article for AOPA, Best talked with a number of airport managers and fixed-base operators around the country to see if they were aware of any problems with the drinking private pilot. Those responses included by Best and AOPA denied any problem existed. But certain comments made by these aviation veterans were indicative in themselves that problems did indeed exist.

Sid Cutter of Cutter Flying Service, Albuquerque, New Mexico, told Best that he considered the drunken pilot a rarity in his area. "Over the years we have on only one or two occasions made a call to the FAA to see if they could get some guy stopped," Cutter said. What he didn't say was that such calls to the FAA are futile in all but the most extreme cases. A pilot would literally have to be falling-down drunk before anyone, including the FAA, could legally take steps to bar him from piloting his own plane.

When asked by Best what he would do if he suspected an outbound pilot was intoxicated, Cutter replied that he'd instruct his boys to run out and park a gas truck in front of the plane. "But you've got to be awfully sure you are right," Cutter added.

John S. Yodice, AOPA's Washington counsel, told Best that even if a pilot had a few drinks but didn't appear intoxicated, he (Yodice) didn't think there was any jurisdiction for taking obstructive action to prevent him from flying his own airplane. Yodice suggested that if a pilot's speech was slurred and his walk unsteady, then you could try to keep him from taking a plane into the air, perhaps even going so far as to taking the pilot's keys and physically preventing him from moving his airplane. Yodice offered this on what he felt was a reasonable assumption that, once the pilot sobered up, he might be appreciative. The message was clear, however. To take such an action placed you in an extremely tenuous legal posture. At best, your position would be a gray one. As Yodice pointed out during his interview with Best, if a drunken pilot was physically restrained, that technically would be battery. If the pilot's keys were taken, that would be considered theft. AOPA's lawyer did say that he couldn't imagine a prosecutor bringing this type of charge, or a person who'd been intoxicated bringing a civil suit on such a claim. At least, Yodice didn't know of any such suits ever being filed. He concluded his interview by telling Best, "I would not hesitate to take reasonable measures to prevent a man from flying while he was drunk—*but I wouldn't have much legal protection.*" [author's italics]

All the men interviewed in Best's article denied a problem existed. But they generally referred to intoxicated pilots, as opposed to drinking pilots. Herein lies the crux of the problem. What is intoxication? And is intoxication really the issue? Isn't the cause for concern the fact that any drinking takes place before flight? Dr. Mohler and the FAA have spent a considerable sum of the taxpayers' money to determine the extent of the problem of pilots drinking before they fly. It has been concluded a problem does exist, in greater proportions than previously realized. The airlines have always recognized the dangers inherent in drinking and flying and hold rigid discipline over their flight personnel. But private aviation fights on successfully to stifle any tightening of the rules.

Perhaps one of the reasons for private aviation's continued success in battling any increased regulation over the drinking habits of private pilots has been the difficulty in translating statistics into meaningful personal involvement. Numbers on a page are not the best way to foster concern. Also, on the surface, Dr. Mohler's findings are not great in terms of the total number of private pilots killed each year. But when it is realized that only fatalities are included in the study, a greater sense of "number" becomes evident. How many pilots, flying after drinking, have managed to bring their aircraft down safely through chance or maximum utilization of skills? How many nonfatal accidents have involved airmen under the influence of alcohol? The fatalities in themselves, significant as they are, do not present the full picture.

As part of its effort to persuade members not to mix bottle with throttle, AOPA runs occasional case histories in *The Pilot*. One involved a private pilot who, after dinner and a few beers with his wife, decided it would be pleasant to view the sunset from aloft. They went to the airport and got in their plane. It wouldn't start. The pilot advanced the throttle about a quarter of an inch, got out, and turned the prop manually. The engine fired and the aircraft proceeded to move across the parking apron, prop turning. The plane headed for planes parked on the apron. The pilot managed to crawl inside the plane and kill the engine. The plane came to rest inches from other aircraft. Fortunately, no one had been standing in the way of the plane as it made its pilotless journey across the apron.

The pilot, in this story, acknowledged that he'd forgotten to set the brake and reset the chocks under the wheels before turning the prop. He also admitted having driven more casually than usual to the airport. His wife had noticed this, too. One wonders what the outcome might have been if he'd made it into the air. It is also interesting that AOPA chose to use his case history to make its point about drinking and flying. Its rebuttal to Dr. Mohler's study defended the airman who has a couple of beers before flight on the grounds that such a small amount of alcohol would not necessarily impair his performance.

Case histories of airman fatalities in which alcohol was

involved are numerous and detailed. Within the past two years, the following have occurred in different areas of the country.

A midwestern businessman, so drunk his speech was slurred in his radio communications with ground control, crashed while attempting to land after many passes at a four-thousand-foot runway.

A private pilot committed suicide by flying his light plane into a university building. His blood alcohol level was 260 mg%.

A forty-one-year-old ranch hand, on parole and working under an alias, buzzed the ranch at which he was employed and crashed. Blood alcohol level: 115 mg%.

A known alcoholic crashed after several low-level passes over his home.

A physician, 43, with a total of seven and half hours of night flying experience, crashed and was killed in the Rocky Mountain area. His blood alcohol level was 44 mg%, which is enough to produce, according to the National Safety Council, "euphoria, increased self-confidence, decreased inhibitions, diminution of attention, judgment and control."

A farmer, after playing cards and drinking with the airport manager from 2 A.M. to 5 A.M., took off and crashed. His blood alcohol level was 270 mg%.

A businessman and his wife left a Connecticut industrial city at 9:30 P.M. after visiting a funeral home. The husband was not instrument rated and didn't bother to ask for a weather briefing. The aircraft crashed shortly after takeoff. Both husband and wife were killed. The toxicological report showed the man's blood alcohol level to be 130 mg%.

A druggist with over five hundred flying hours crashed in the Far West. Accident investigators listed the probable cause as the pilot's inefficiency and lack of judgment due to alcoholic impairment. His blood alcohol level was 120 mg%.

A lawyer and three companions had dinner and, according to witnesses at the restaurant, three rounds of drinks before taking a cab to a California airport at 9 P.M. They'd flown in to that same airport to have dinner; it is one of the busiest airports in the nation. The wreckage of their aircraft was found the following morning. All four men were dead. No flight plan had been filed nor had weather been checked. The pilot did not have even one hour of instrument flight time.

An insurance executive flew his aircraft erratically and crashed. Witnesses who had spoken with him immediately prior to his takeoff testified, "His speech was slurred, his walk uncertain, and he appeared to be under the influence of drugs or alcohol." A postmortem showed his blood alcohol level to be 190 mg%.

The list goes on. In a surprisingly high number of cases, the pilots involved were experienced, at least in comparison to the average experience level of private pilots. They were, for the most part, men and women with above average education and job skills. And each of the case histories recounted in this chapter occurred after Dr. Mohler's study was released to the public. The education programs conducted by the FAA and AOPA to teach the private pilot about the dangers of drinking and flying evidently were totally ineffectual where these people were concerned. Self-preservation was also absent.

Attempts to elicit a clear-cut and definitive answer to the question, "Why hasn't the FAA or NTSB pushed for a strong drinking regulation for private pilots?" are generally met with vague and irrelevant responses. I first asked Ralph Lovering and Dr. Mervin K. Strickler of the FAA about it.

LOVERING: How would you determine or how would you control an individual taking a drink? How would you control the amount of alcohol an individual has taken or the effect it might have on him, even with an eight- or twelve-hour lapse rule between drinking and flying?

REPORTER: Then why do the airlines have such a rule?"

LOVERING: That's just company practice.

REPORTER: I know that. But they do it for reasons of

safety, don't they? That's why they bother, isn't it. They don't just do it for fun.

STRICKLER: Do you know whether it works or not?

REPORTER: I understand it does work.

STRICKLER: Have you ever heard of a captain being penalized for drinking?

REPORTER: Yes.

STRICKLER: You've touched on a horrendous problem.

LOVERING: A social problem. How do you handle it?

REPORTER: Maybe by ruling against it where pilots are concerned. At least the individual knows the consequences of his act before he does it. He knows he can be severely penalized if caught and lose his flying privilege. At least the airport manager or another pilot can stop him from going up and be legally sound in doing that.

STRICKLER: I think the problem of drinking is the same as the problem of drug addiction in our society.

REPORTER: I'm sure it is. But I wonder if that matters in this matter of aviation and—"

STRICKLER: Many of us here in the FAA feel we have the responsibility to let the airman know the consequences of certain acts purely from a physiological and operational point of view. On the assumption that the bulk of private pilots are reasonably rational, and they are, we feel that education is the most . . ."

I also posed the question to C. O. Miller, director of the Bureau of Aviation Safety, National Transportation Safety Board.

MILLER: Let's understand each other. There is a Federal Air Regulation that brings up this subject about flying under the influence of alcohol. I have the personal opinion that you have to draw the line somewhere in protecting a man against himself. We could construct a rule having to do with milligrams of alcohol and stuff like that. But isn't this really a situation where it's up to the individual himself?

REPORTER: It is if he were the only one involved. But I think of it in terms of myself as an airline passenger. I'm very much at the mercy of the drinking private pilot.

MILLER: I think you'll find that the commercial carriers have a rule that their pilots can't drink before flying.

REPORTER: I know that. I'm talking about being at the mercy of the drinking private pilot who might conflict with the airliner I'm flying on.

MILLER: The basic question here is to what degree does the federal government go in regulating this? This is an area of basic political philosophy. It so happens I'm an old conservative from California. I would prefer to see the federal government come in and control only where breakdowns occur.

REPORTER: But the FAA study indicated that 30 percent of the private aviation fatalities had blood alcohol levels above that which would have impaired their judgment and performance. Isn't this a pretty serious breakdown?

MILLER: I think we lead ourselves down the primrose path looking for a factor that produces accidents. This is the tone in which most people have treated the alcohol problem. Accidents are a combination of events. Overemphasis on a single cause in a single accident is, in my humble opinion, one of the most serious problems facing us in the accident prevention field today. It muddies the waters.

REPORTER: Isn't it true that most private aviation accidents have to do with lack of pilot judgment? Couldn't alcohol have contributed to this lack of judgment?

MILLER: Again, you're looking for a single cause. You fell into the trap of assessing a factor as being identified with an accident. A friend of mine on the West Coast was telling me about how they're trying to tell people not to drink before they drive. Real great. And then somebody decided to teach them how to drive when they're drunk. I think there's a limit to the point where you can influence the attitudes and behavior of people. There comes a time when you have to accept people driving while they're drunk and what do you do? Let's teach them to drive while they're drunk.

REPORTER: Let me ask you this directly. You don't feel that a regulation should be enacted by the FAA prohibiting drinking for a certain number of hours before flying?

MILLER: I don't feel close enough to the problem to answer that directly. I'm afraid I can't answer that.

Of the officials I spoke with, only Dr. Mohler seemed willing to acknowledge a problem did, in fact, exist with the drinking airman.

"The only rule we have now," he told me, "is that the pilot will not be under the influence of alcohol. We've had this rule for many years. This is where the NTSB is in a quandry. A pilot can say he had three martinis but say he wasn't influenced by them. And, of course, as you go higher in altitude and less oxygen is available, you have a double impairment."

Congress has, at times, broached the drinking question in certain of its aviation hearings. General William F. McKee, administrator of the FAA during the period of July and August, 1967, when the Committee on Interstate and Foreign Commerce and the Subcommittee on Transportation and Aeronautics held aviation safety hearings, was asked by Ohio Congressman Samuel L. Devine, "Is drinking by pilots in general aviation at this time considered to be a major safety hazard? Has it grown to any proportions that you have great concern about this problem?"

McKEE: I don't think, Mr. Devine, that it is major, but we do have a problem there, and I think that everybody recognizes it, and that is the reason that we are conducting, and so are the various associations, a very vigorous educational campaign as to what is involved when a pilot takes a drink before he takes off, or a few hours before he takes off. We do consider it a problem.

DEVINE: Not a major one at this time?

McKEE: I will say it is a significant problem. I wouldn't call it a major problem.

Congressman Devine dropped it at that point.

These same hearings produced the following dialogue between Baltimore Congressman Samuel N. Friedel and General McKee. David D. Thomas, deputy administrator of the FAA under McKee and the man who succeeded McKee as administrator, was also called into the discussion.

FRIEDEL: I have received some mail about aircraft accidents caused by pilot drinking. For the record, will you tell us about any regulations prohibiting pilots from drinking before takeoff?

McKEE: They are quite extensive and spelled out. That has been a major subject of concern to us, and I will ask Mr. Moore or Mr. Thomas to spell out the regulations.

THOMAS: Mr. Friedel, most of the airlines have their own rules, and most of them prohibit drinking for twenty-four hours before a trip, and as far as I know, these rules are quite rigidly followed. In the case of general aviation, there is the normal legal regulation against operating under the influence of—that is alcohol or drugs, or any other adverse effect. There is no particular provision as to the number of hours before the flight. We tried number of hours once, but enforcing it, actually finding out whether or not they did drink within a certain time period, is almost impossible and also, the varying effect of the amount of the drink and what it was is difficult to determine. So we rely on operating under the influence.

FRIEDEL: Well, I understand the commercial pilots are

watched very rigidly, and there is no question in my mind that they are all right. But in general aviation, in so many hundreds of airports all over the country where they don't have towers or anything, is there any thought being given to how they could be regulated?

THOMAS: Yes, sir, we have given it a lot of thought, but this is an extremely difficult one to enforce, or actually detect, whether or not they have been drinking, so we have gone the education route, or designated medical examiners to give out the information on the difficulty of flying after drinking, and particularly the effect of oxygen, which is cumulative over the longer effects of drinking. But principally, we are trying to get at it by education, and enforcement is extremely difficult because we do not want to follow the pilot, or have no way of following him immediately before he takes off."

Congressman Friedel was either dazzled with confusion or lost interest; he dropped the line of questioning and went on to other things.

Later in the aviation safety hearings, Congressman Clarence J. Brown, Jr., of Ohio, again brought up the drinking subject. He questioned both General McKee and Bobbie R. Allen, director of the Bureau of Safety, NTSB.

BROWN: Let me ask you one other question related to a question asked earlier, and that is on the matter of alcohol. In the case of the Hendersonville or Asheville crash [that accident occurred close to both cities in North Carolina], how are you going to find out if alcohol was a factor?

ALLEN: Are you relating this to crew members, sir?

BROWN: I am relating it to anybody who might be involved in the significant safety aspects of this accident.

ALLEN: The only time we conduct tests for alcohol is in the case of a deceased pilot, crew member, and we do not obtain blood samples from people who survived an accident.

BROWN: Is there any way in the policing of FAA regulations that such factors are checked on a regular or intermittent or spot check basis?"

ALLEN: I am not sure I understand your question.

BROWN: Such factors as the health factor, possibility of flying while under the influence, and so forth. Are there regulations which prohibit this?

ALLEN: Well, the regulation, I think, as Mr. Thomas pointed out earlier, is prohibition against flying under the influence.

BROWN: That is right. Now, does anyone know whether there are any pilots in the air at the moment flying under the influence, unless they have a crash?

ALLEN: I don't think that you would know, sir.

BROWN: There is no way of policing this problem?

ALLEN: Policing of that particular type of regulation would be a tremendous task.

Falling back on the difficulties of policing any new and needed regulations is a common practice of both the FAA and AOPA. And Congress has usually been willing to accept this excuse.

After some discussion on whether it would be feasible to build commercial aircraft so strong that they could withstand midair collisions—Allen thought they probably could but would never get off the ground—the alcohol discussion was resumed.

ALLEN: Now, when you get into the subject of alcohol, which is a problem, I just don't know how to police it. We do have occasional reports from people that this rule has been violated, and upon getting reports we immediately make an investigation, but it is very hard to control.

BROWN: Some effort was apparently made to police the two navy planes [referring to a midair collision between two navy aircraft], but there is no spot check done of general aviation.

McKEE: You mean when we have an accident?

BROWN: No. Under normal conditions, routine procedures, occasional spot check, or either.

McKEE: Go up to, say, Mr. Brown flying a private airplane from Dayton, Ohio, to Washington, and what do you think would happen if I sent an aviation inspector out to find out if Mr. Brown had been drinking before flying his airplane?

The hearings were ended moments later.

The final comment by General McKee is quite meaningful. It sums up the underlying absurdity of all discussion on the drinking-flying problem. The private pilot, secure in a long history of inalienable rights, would not take kindly to an FAA inspector inquiring into his drinking habits prior to flight. The inspector would have no legal justification for making such an inquiry under the existing regulation. All discussion takes on a certain useless dimension without the needed basic change in the regulation.

At no time during the safety hearings did Dr. Mohler's study come up, either in the questioning or the testimony. That so thorough and significant a study could be conducted at taxpayer expense and not play a part in hearings on aviation safety can lead an observer down many paths of conclusion. The FAA does not feel that drinking and flying constitutes a "major problem." Semantics. Perhaps in the broad spectrum of the aviation safety system it does not indicate a "major problem." But with over 80 percent of private aviation accidents attributed to pilot error-lack of judgment, it is reasonable to ask whether alcohol is playing a part in these accidents and contributing to error and bad judgment. Dr. Mohler's study does, of course, add weight to this reason.

The air traffic controllers, about whom enough good things

cannot be said, seldom venture viewpoints on intra-industry battles. The controllers are charged with the positive and safe control of all aircraft in the skies. Aircraft are handled on a first-come, first-served basis under present regulations. The controllers are having enough trouble getting the men and improved equipment they need to make the current ATC system work without taking sides in the airline-private aviation squabble. But significant practical insight can be gained into the day-to-day conditions in our skies by talking off the record with controllers. One, now a supervisor, told me of two cases in which he had talked drunken pilots down to relatively safe landings.

"One was a doctor, I remember," he told me, "who was so drunk he didn't know he was flying in descending circles in the middle of the LaGuardia Airport landing pattern. He had a damn tough time talking, and how he actually made his landing is a tribute to somebody someplace, I guess."

The controller went on to tell me of the other case in which he had helped a drunk pilot bring his plane down for a landing. This occurred over Pennsylvania. After an hour of radio communication with the pilot, lost above the clouds, the controller managed to talk him down to a local airfield. The pilot crashed however, during the landing, destroying his plane and suffering bruises.

Personal reports such as these are common in the aviation business. But firsthand accounts, documented accident findings, and reports such as Dr. Mohler's do not, in the bureaucratic mind of the FAA, constitute a major problem. Perhaps Congressman Rosenthal was right. Perhaps nothing *will* be done until a drunken seventeen-year-old kid in a private plane smacks into an airline jet loaded with people over Brooklyn. And although to say that such an occurrence will be too late is cliché, it seems the only fitting conclusion to which one can come.

CHAPTER SIX

Who Pays?

Who pays the bills for the nation's airway systems and the
bulk of airport costs? Basically, it's you and I, those of us
who fly on the nation's scheduled airlines.

The *Boston Globe*
September 8, 1968

Like the wealthy uncle supporting a shiftless nephew with no
strings attached, the airline passengers of the United States
pay the bills and say nothing. They provide the bulk of revenue
for the support and improvement of the airways/airport system
through the payment of the 5 percent excise tax on airline
tickets. In 1967, airline passengers paid $203 million into
the United States Treasury through this tax. In 1968, the
figure rose to $224 million. And legislation is currently before
Congress to increase the tax rate. But even without an increase
in the percentage paid by the passenger, the growth of commercial aviation will insure an increase in the total money
paid by passengers on commercial airlines. The FAA estimates
that in 1969, assuming no increase in the excise tax percentage comes out of Congress, passengers will pay $249.4 million.
These estimates project into 1972 when passenger contributions will be in excess of $350 million.

The airlines use 44 percent of the airways system. The money generated by the passenger excise tax is almost equal to the airlines' allocated fair share of the cost of the system.

Private aviation uses about 28 percent of the airways system. Its fair share of the cost would be approximately $150 million a year. It pays $6 million a year, or 4 percent of its allocated share. FAA estimates project private aviation's contribution in 1969 to be $8.3 million, still 4 percent of its fair share as the costs of operating the system rise.

The figures above represent the hard fiscal facts. But, despite such facts, the Aircraft Owners and Pilots Association made the following statement before the Aviation Subcommittee of the Senate Committee on Commerce in June, 1968. The hearings were held to discuss the proposed Airport Development Act of 1968, and the statement was delivered by Joseph B. Hartranft, president of AOPA.

"Some government bureaucrats and airline spokesmen have advanced the fallacious allegation that general aviation is not paying its way. Let me set the record straight. General aviation is the only one that is paying its way and more. Let no one, however exalted his station, convince you differently."

Members of the Congress of the United States are extremely busy men. A myriad of matters comes to their attention, each to be weighed, considered, and acted upon in the best possible combination of reason, knowledge, and concern. No one expects all members of Congress to become expert in all fields, aviation included. But with the dollars-and-cents facts so readily available, one wonders at those members of Congress who accept Hartranft's allegations. The president of AOPA has, of course, various malleable statistical material with which to work in defense of his claim. But as in all cases of misused statistics and deceptive use of fact, the basic story can be found beneath the rubble of finesse. Again, a hat must be tipped to private aviation and its ability to persuade.

Money is the key to curing aviation's ills. Big money. Airports become obsolete as the opening day ribbon is cut at the entrance gate. The air traffic control system, brittle and cracking under the weight of increased use, is no longer capable of handling aviation's stunning growth. Air traffic controllers, joyous over a new FAA rule cutting their work day to ten hours, extend themselves far beyond the bounds of reasonable human tolerance and capability. Roads to airports are jammed. New aircraft, bigger and faster, turn formerly adequate runways into inadequate parking ramps. Huge airliners belch out the baggage of four hundred passengers. People stand shoulder to shoulder in terminal buildings damned in the past for being too spacious and far-flung. And overhead, subsonic and supersonic jets circle a thousand feet above each other, the delicate line of separation known to the controllers on the ground only by what each pilot tells them on the radio. The big jets circle as far north as Montreal. They string out three hundred miles to the west. They stack over the Atlantic. Over Norfolk, Virginia. They circle for hours, each waiting to be lowered one step—one thousand feet—to the next rung on the ladder of descent. Thousands of people fume on the ground as passengers they are to meet circle aimlessly overhead. The delays are felt around the world. Flights are canceled in Los Angeles and Madrid because the aircraft are still in New York. *This* is aviation today at the larger hub areas. To accurately forecast the future is simply to increase the effect. It is, to quote an air traffic controller, "one hell of a mess."

Money *is* the key. And guts, the guts to discard false, twisted, and misleading claims uttered in self-interest. And time-honored but outdated principles and rules must be reexamined and reevaluated.

Who should pay?

No one wants to pay more than his fair share of anything. It is relatively simple in most cases to assign fair share; matrons at Wednesday lunch manage to define individual cost to the penny. But to determine the fair share for each user of the nation's airways/airports system is not so easily accomplished.

Even without private aviation's clouding of the issue, arriving at a fair share formula takes groundwork, imagination, and even social evaluation.

There has always been a wide gap between the annual cost of operating and improving the airways system and the revenue collected from the users of the system—the airlines, private aviation, and the military. This gap has been filled by revenue from the general tax fund of the U.S. Treasury. There is good, sound argument why the general taxpayer, although he may never set foot on an airplane, should pay toward the maintenance of the air travel system. Aviation benefits everyone. Air travel has allowed business to expand and diversify far faster and more efficiently than when ground transportation formed the only link between communities. An airport can turn a stagnant area into a prospering one. In the 1940s, 90 percent of industrial expansion took place within metropolitan areas. Today, 80 percent of the nation's industrial expansion takes place outside these metropolitan areas. Aviation, in all forms, has made this possible.

However, the prevailing fiscal mood of the federal government has been one in which, although the distinct benefit of aviation to the nation at large is recognized, further taxation of non-participants is frowned upon. The pressing costs of international involvement and domestic crises prohibit any further taxation of the nation for programs capable of self-support.

The airlines, in their evaluation of this mood in Washington, feel that benefits derived by the general public should be deducted from the cost of the airways/airports system before the users—airlines, private aviation, and military—are assessed their fair shares.

Private aviation feels that the public benefit is so great, and that its (private aviation's) needs are so small in use of the system, that it is already paying more than its fair share.

Faced with today's aviation crisis, the federal government must act. It must provide increased monetary aid with which the air traffic control system can be improved and manned to meet the increased demands made on it, and to hurry the needed development of new and improved airport facilities. The sums necessary to accomplish these objectives are staggering. It is estimated that expenditures for domestic airways improvements, operations, and maintenance for the five-year period of fiscal year 1969 through 1973 will amount to $5.5 billion. Of this, $1.1 billion is allocated as the military's fair share of the cost, leaving $4.4 billion to be paid by the civil users of the system. (It should be kept in mind that the $5.5 billion figure is for the airways system alone; it does not include the cost of airport development and/or improvement.)

In airport development, it is estimated that $2 billion will be needed for the same five-year period used in the airways estimate. This figure is for airport development and improvements excluding hangars, terminals, and other passenger and cargo-handling facilities. The government's best estimate for terminal and other passenger facility requirements for the same period is between $1.5 and $2 billion.

The need for vast new sums of money is the result of grossly bad planning on the government's part. There can be no excuse for the inadequate and inappropriate preparation leading to today's aviation trial. In the face of obvious growth, the FAA, CAB, and Congress have never acknowledged aviation's needs of tomorrow. This is not, of course, unique with aviation. History has proved that too many things must reach crisis proportions before action is taken in Washington. However, in regard to aviation, not only have the FAA, Congress, and other involved agencies failed to keep pace, they have actually cut back on systems capability and manpower. They have treated the aviation industry as one that is losing ground rather than gaining ground with each passing month.

The Civil Aeronautics Authority, the FAA's predecessor, was never an agency to take charge and move forward with any aggressiveness. Timid in going to the Administration or Congress for funds, the CAA suffered for its lack of drive. In fiscal 1956, two years before Congress rammed through the creation of the FAA, President Dwight D. Eisenhower's Bureau of the Budget allocated the CAA only $162 million as a total budget. A scant $20 million of this went for air traffic control equipment, and less than $2 million went into equipment research and development. This brand of economy, practiced every year by the CAA, did nothing to close the gap between the system and the traffic it was to control.

The FAA got off to a fine start in 1958. General Elwood R. Quesada, the first administrator, went after and received large increases in the budget. By 1960, the FAA's budget had quadrupled over that of the CAA. Its work force had doubled. Quesada used a firm hand in dealing with the various members of the aviation community. He even tightened the FAA control of air traffic, a move that brought anguished cries from the private aviation sector of the industry. Joseph B. Hartranft, AOPA's president, greeted General Quesada's departure from the FAA at the end of the Eisenhower Administration with, "The Quesada type of uninhibited rule making and ironfisted enforcement has contributed little to safety, despite the availability of almost unlimited funds and personnel."

Quesada replied by saying, "Hartranft and two or three other top officials of AOPA have engaged in a calculated program of invective and distortion to vilify the FAA. They have done this to incite a false sense of grievance among private pilots, and then make an unabashed appeal for more members and membership fees."

Clearly, AOPA and private aviation were glad to see General Quesada leave the FAA. Now it remained to be seen what changes the new Administration would bring to official Washington and aviation.

For the most part, everyone in the aviation community was pleased with the choice of Najeeb Halaby as new administrator of the FAA. While Quesada had centralized power in aviation, Halaby would tend to decentralize the power and decision-making process and give them back to the industry. A man who wanted to be liked, Halaby proceeded with a soft hand through his days as chief of the nation's aviation agency. He displayed a willingness to bend, too much so for a number of people.

Najeeb Halaby believed in the use of study groups for problem solving. In his first year at the helm of the FAA, Halaby appointed no fewer than eleven panels to study various aspects of aviation and report their conclusions to the administrator. There was much advice during the Halaby reign at the FAA, much more than action. During a House hearing to investigate pilot laxity, held in 1962 and chaired by Congressman Jack Brooks of Texas, Halaby asked Brooks if he, Halaby, should be strict in judging witnesses before the committee who had testified that they'd helped pilots violate the regulations of the CAA.

Brooks replied, "Well, my judgment is that it is your responsibility. I am not the administrator of the FAA. My judgments are made on votes. I record that vote. The people in my district decide whether I should be returned to office. The manner in which you conduct your office is the one which determines whether or not you are returned there. That is the chance you take."

"Yes, sir," Halaby replied.

At one point later in those hearings, Halaby introduced a list of enforcement actions taken by the FAA against pilots and other crew members of commercial airlines. He added with pride that he was responsible for a rule prohibiting drunken passengers from flying on airline aircraft. He told the committee, "I would like to bring to your attention the rules I have promulgated in the last year against drunks on board airplanes. We have tightened the rules up very strictly. I have fined men one thousand, five hundred, and two hundred dollars for boarding aircraft while drunk and disturbing the peace."

Because of Najeeb Halaby, passengers are not allowed to be drunk when they board an airliner. That's good. Nor are passengers allowed more than two drinks while on board, nor are they allowed to carry liquor on board and drink it. Those things, too, are good. But the private pilot, the man at the controls of an aircraft, is still allowed to drink before, and even during, flight. That subject never came up in those 1962 hearings.

Administrator Halaby called for a "lean, clean agency" when he took over the leadership of the FAA. He called for this in the face of air traffic increasing at the rate of 15 percent a year. Research and development programs were shelved under his lean and clean policy. The Oklahoma City school for air traffic controllers was closed. The agency stopped hiring new controllers. In 1960, under General Quesada, the FAA's budget for air traffic control equipment had reached $107 million. By 1967, this figure had dropped to $27 million, as the FAA continued along its lean, clean lines.

In 1963, twelve thousand controllers handled 29 million takeoffs and landings. In 1967, fourteen thousand controllers handled 50 million takeoffs and landings. General "Bozo" McKee, by this time administrator of the FAA and of the Halaby fiscal school, commented, "We felt we could handle the additional workload by working our people a little harder."

In July, 1966, during which the nation's major airports were handling traffic at record rates—Kennedy Airport alone handled 1,668 takeoffs and landings on July 1 for a new record—a supervisor at the New York Traffic Control Center in Islip, New York, received a cash bonus and letter of recommendation for coming up with a formula for reducing the number of personnel at the Islip center. At the time, the facility was undermanned. It still is.

Air traffic controller Mike Rock testified at the House hearings on government operations in August, 1968, hearings called to investigate the emergency situation confronting the ATC system.

ROCK: One hundred twenty-eight aircraft have been handled at LaGuardia. LaGuardia has two runways. It is mathematically impossible with VFR and IFR together—I don't care if it is the clearest day in the world—to run it by the book and move that many airplanes. I had 117 myself. I have landed three airplanes on the same runway at the same time against the book while the supervisors were cheering, "Keep going, Mike, give them some more." And this is a fact. At the Indianapolis Center they gave this guy a nice plaque because he handled 60 airplanes on his frequency. There is not a man alive that can handle 60 airplanes on his frequency and do it safely. But they congratulated him.

Congressman John W. Wydler of New York questioned Rock on threats made on controllers' jobs during the 1968 controller slowdown.

WYDLER: Was it true that your air traffic controller jobs were threatened as reported in the newspapers?

ROCK: Yes, it is true. The area manager from New York called the controllers that were coming on duty for the three-to-eleven shift for a meeting prior to the shift starting.

WYDLER: Where was this?

ROCK: At the common IFR room in New York. He told them unless the traffic increased more or less back to the old days that "we are going to be missing a few air traffic controllers in Kennedy." He stated later on television, I believe, that he didn't say this. We have the signatures of the controllers that were in the room when this statement was made. He read this statement or gave this statement. He did not stay around to ask—to have the controllers ask him—what he meant by this. He left the room and there was no exchange between the controllers and the area manager. Then he said [later] that he meant they should be transferred. We have over five hundred air traffic controllers in the New York area who accepted his offer for a transfer. They want out. And that is the story of that.

Congress is now more aware than ever of the crisis in our skies. The tactic used in the summer of 1968 by the controllers in slowing down and handling traffic by the book brought this awareness to Congress. And it spurred the elected representatives to some action. The FAA had requested $70 million for facilities and equipment in fiscal 1969. This represented a 30 percent increase over fiscal 1968. It also represented another example of a woefully inadequate budget request. Congress, always reluctant to give the FAA much money, based upon past performance by the agency in utilizing the funds, chopped the figure to $65 million. Then, in the heat of 1968's congested summer, Congress upped the figure to $120 million. The controllers' action had reaped very definite tangible changes in funding the aviation system.

But even this increase in funds for equipment and control facilities does not represent a substantial attack on the problem. Rather, it is a weak, although welcome, staying action. Despite this congressional increase in facilities and equipment funds, the actual FAA budget for fiscal 1969 is more than $200 million less than requested by the agency. The fiscal '69 budget is over $62 million less than the budget for fiscal 1968. One of the prime areas slashed for 1969 was the grants-in-aid program for airports. The appropriation for this program is $70 million for 1969. The FAA requested $65 million for fiscal 1970. The House of Representatives slashed this request to nothing—literally zero. The Senate restored it to $65 million. Conference compromises took away $35 million, leaving $30 million for airport aid in fiscal 1970. This figure, too, is a token staying action in the face of increased needs. As the experts agree, congestion in the skies is the result of a lack of concrete on the ground, the term concrete referring to runways. Such cuts in aid programs to the nation's airports do little to solve the aviation ills of the day, to say nothing of keeping pace with growth. The systems approach to aviation demands that each step and segment of the system be improved. There can be no improvement in aviation unless the *system* and all its parts are considered and acted upon aggressively and in concert.

One cannot fault the Congress for its reluctance to give the FAA much money. Members of Congress have stated on occasion that since the FAA spends its money so poorly anyway, there is little sense in giving the agency very much to squander. This attitude on the part of Congress, although justified from one point of view, will not do much to solve the aviation problem. Its thinking is understandable, but not defendable.

One example of the FAA's ability to spend money without much to show for it concerns its bird study of the mid-sixties, now becoming a classic for collectors of government trivia. The agency had set out to study birds and the hazards they presented to aircraft. Staff members of the FAA charted bird flight patterns and characteristics and determined, in their words, "geese are considered the greatest hazard to aircraft because of their abundance, large size, occurrence in large flocks, relatively slow flight and high altitude of flight." The FAA experts went on to categorize over fifty types of birds, listing them in relative order of hazard to aircraft. Also included in the findings was a detailed analysis of migratory patterns of classes of birds, this section included presumably to inform pilots of routes to be avoided at various times of the year when the birds were winging north or south at assigned altitudes.

With all this FAA attention directed toward the birds, it's little wonder that Congressman Brooks of Texas, in making his opening statement at the April, 1966, hearings on government operations, said, "The FAA has long warned pilots of the danger of bird strikes—particularly Canada geese. Why then did the FAA approve construction of a large jet airport only a mile or less from a 38,000-acre wildlife refuge inhabited four months of the year or more by more than 100,000 Canada geese and ducks?"

General "Bozo" McKee, FAA administrator, answered the Texas congressman's question in two ways. First, as most leaders of federal agencies are prone to do, he made a general statement in defense of himself and the agency.

McKEE: I would like to deviate from my prepared statement for a moment to tell the committee that a year ago when the President of the United States asked me to come over to the White House and asked me to take this job, the first thing he said to me was, "Safety, Bozo, is your number one priority. Do you understand that?" And I said, "Yes, sir." And I've never forgotten it.

McKee then proceeded to speak with pride of the cost cutting programs at the FAA, programs that have contributed to the chaos in the skies today.

McKEE: In August, 1963, we had a total of 46,656 employees. At the end of March, 1966, our employment had declined to 43,330—a reduction of more than 3,300 employees. Excluding the supersonic transport program, the FAA 1967 budget request is nearly $51 million less than our appropriations for 1966. In fact, we are seeking less money in 1967 than was appropriated to us in 1961. All of these reductions in employment and budget have been in face of the explosive growth of aviation activity and agency workload which I described earlier in my statement.

Congressman Brooks managed to get everyone back on the original bird question and the construction of the new jetport at Huntsville, Alabama.

BROOKS: In February, Mr. Thomas [assistant administrator of the FAA], 1964, did the Interior Department Fish and Wildlife Service not notify the FAA in Atlanta that the location of this new airport would constitute a serious hazard to aircraft?

THOMAS: They did, sir . . . they asked that we consider it if we had not already considered it.

Some conversation ensued concerning the needs of Huntsville for a new airport and about the search project that had been undertaken to select a proper site. Congressman Brooks again asked whether the FAA truly considered the problem of Canada geese in the Huntsville area when it approved construction of the new airport. He referred to his notes and added the following question.

BROOKS: Did the FAA get a letter from the GAO [General Accounting Office] requesting information as to the extent of your evaluation and the feasibility of the FAA extending its site selection criteria to include consideration of greater than normal bird hazards?

THOMAS: Yes, sir, we have such a letter.

BROOKS: Have you answered it?

THOMAS: No, sir, we have not, because we are looking into the facts. It is a draft report.

Thomas then asked if he could continue with what he had to say about the birds. Congressman Brooks agreed he could continue with his statement.

THOMAS: At the peak of the migratory season we have had them [birds] up to fourteen thousand feet in height, but generally speaking we can expect migration to occur, that is, the peak to occur in altitudes, say, from four thousand to six thousand feet in the fall and spring when they [birds] are going back and forth. Our biggest problem is with starlings and pigeons. We do consider geese extremely hazardous because of their large size. We do have strikes with them. But in looking at this earlier here specifically—

BROOKS: You did think that Canada geese were the greatest hazard to aircraft, did you not?

THOMAS: Due to their size. If you look back in history, the whistling swan and starlings are the ones that caused the two accidents [Boston and Ellicott City, Maryland]. But if you take the population, there are 400,000 or 500,000

Canada geese that migrate every year. They are large. There are quite a few of them in here (*referring to the Huntsville area map*).

Some discussion ensued about a military base that had been in the Huntsville area during World War I. No one could remember the name of the base. The bird testimony resumed.

THOMAS: We find from the agricultural pilots who work with ducks and geese that the ducks and geese, when they are resting and feeding, are not disturbed by airplanes unless the airplanes get down to about fifty feet above the water. Motorboats go back and forth and do not disturb them. The problem here is whether they will be involved in the feeding areas. Traffic patterns are handled and population—

BROOKS: Mr. Thomas, what I am pointing out is that the birds are going to fly from the main concentration right behind you to the east, to the other area, both the center and on the far eastern part of the refuge, and they will fly back in the west to sack in for the night. But they are going to be flying back and forth, and these birds do not always stay where you tell them.

THOMAS: No, sir, they do not.

BROOKS: Maybe they do not understand so well. They generally fly about seventy yards from you, I find, just on the edge.

THOMAS: Yes, sir.

McKEE: Beyond shotgun range.

THOMAS: Every hunter we talk to says altitude—

BROOKS: Seventy yards is about the standard altitude— they kind of wave their wings at you.

THOMAS: Sixty yards.

BROOKS: As they go by.

THOMAS: Which is slightly above the treetop level. On simulated takeoffs they are easily over twenty-five hundred feet over here *(referring to the map)* and six hundred on landings.

BROOKS: What I want to point out is they fly back and forth. If they had a feed area in the middle, a feed area close to there *(pointing)*, it does compound your problem. The odds go up. Is that what you seem to feel?

THOMAS: No, sir. What I was trying to say is that this is the heaviest concentration, and I talked to both pilots and the hunters.

BROOKS: Yes.

The bird testimony went on the rest of the morning session of the hearings. The end result seemed to be—and no one can really be certain just what was the end result—that, based upon talks with hunters in the area, the geese would not, in all likelihood, fly up high enough to endanger too many airplanes using the new Huntsville jetport. The formal FAA bird study, which included such research projects as firing fifty-nine species of birds from guns at the agency's Atlantic City test site and studying their destructive effects on parked aircraft, seemed to play little part in the final Huntsville decision. The FAA acknowledged that it could have prevented the construction of the new jetport by withholding the federal funds used for the work— $4.5 million. The bird study would seem to have indicated that course of action. But the hunters prevailed, to the surprise of Congressman Brooks. He asked Thomas when the FAA would conclude its studies as to how aircraft might avoid birds in the Huntsville area.

THOMAS: It will be this fall after the birds get back.

Congress has been critical of the FAA on a number of counts through the years. One involves the agency's own fleet of aircraft, which numbered 101 at last count, during the latter part of 1968. Congressman Fletcher Thompson of Georgia, an experienced private pilot and AOPA member, assailed the FAA in 1968 for what he felt were extravagant and unnecessary expenditures for this fleet of aircraft, which range from single-engine piston aircraft to advanced and sophisticated jet planes. In his charges, Thompson accused the FAA of spending over $31 million in 1967 and 1968 for upkeep on the aircraft alone. He cited a case in which an eighty-three passenger Boeing 727, one of the jets owned and operated by the FAA, was used to transport twenty-six women on a public relations trip between Oklahoma City, Washington, and Atlanta. The flight was listed by the FAA as a training flight.

Thompson also charged that, in addition to the FAA's own fleet of aircraft, it had spent over $250,000 on leased aircraft in 1967 and over $3 million in the past three years on open market aircraft rental.

At another time in 1968, Thompson also took aim at a new jet aircraft that had been delivered to the Department of Transportation by the Grumman Aircraft Engineering Corporation. It was a Grumman Gulfstream II, and the initial cost to DOT was $2,876,486, of which $162,181 was designated for what Thompson termed "the most lavish airplane interior available." What particularly riled Thompson was the fact that DOT officials sent the aircraft back for improvements in the interior. These improvements cost $41,848. After the improvements had been completed, Thompson called the aircraft "plushier than superplush." He went on to call the craft "a flying palace."

Various officials at DOT denied any excess spending for the airplane, which had been purchased to provide transportation for department officials instead of their having to use commercial airlines. One spokesman did say the new plane was not "a flying boxcar."

Congressman Thompson's final bit of annoyance came when he was unable to get from the General Accounting Office any complete information on the FAA's expenditures for its aircraft fleet and its operation. The GAO claimed that the FAA did not have uniform cost-reporting systems for its aircraft operations.

To this, Thompson replied by terming the situation "incomprehensible and inexcusable."

Such incidents are unfortunate. Because of them and such futilities as the bird study, the FAA has placed itself in a precarious and weak position with the Congress. Clearly, the FAA is the only governmental body charged with air safety. To insure this safety, it must request and receive great sums of money from the legislative branch, money to be spent on the most-needed improvements in the overall air safety systems concept. And this money must be used on the basis of clear and objective thinking of the gathered experts, without sensitivity to outside pressures, so often imposed in the interests of self-gain. Presently, the FAA is not free of such pressure. And it cannot count on anything from the Congress of the United States. Members of the House and Senate are openly scornful of the FAA's track record in forecasting and acting upon the ills of aviation. Because it has placed itself in such a position with Congress, the FAA is open to what amounts to congressional blackmail from individual members of the House and Senate who champion the cause of self-interest groups. The FAA is weak, and to be weak in Washington is to be vulnerable.

While the FAA waddles in its pool of inefficiency and faces problems by claiming no such problems exist, the Department of Transportation has stepped in and attempted to assume a role of action and clarity. It is the DOT that has estimated the sums needed in the next five years to keep pace with aviation's growth. It is the DOT that has recognized the need to separate aircraft in high-density zones and has gone on record in this matter. It is the DOT that has asked that priority be given to the millions of airline passengers over a small number of special-interest individuals—private pilots.

It is rare that private aviation and the airlines agree on anything. In the case of the DOT's proposed legislation under which the users of the airways/airports system would bear all costs, both private aviation and the airlines have come out in favor of a portion of these costs being borne by the general taxpaying public. It is unlikely they will see their position prevail. The Administration is aware of the limits on increased general taxation, especially in such activities as aviation in which the majority of the citizenry do not participate directly. Ideally, the public should contribute to aviation in this country. But few matters can be solved with ideal solutions. The airlines themselves, although attempting to get their share of the costs cut as much as possible, have generally conceded the inevitability of a complete user-supported system. Paying their share is not foreign to the nation's airlines. Since going off government subsidy after their formative years, the major airlines have, through the passenger ticket tax, contributed what the FAA and DOT consider is an amount roughly equal to benefits received from the system. But private aviation spokesmen claim the airlines pay nothing for their use of the system. With their backs to the wall, private aviation makes a case of the fact that the passengers pay, not the airlines. This is true, but hardly relevant. Taken literally, it follows that the nation's airline passengers should therefore dictate policy direction, instead of private aviation's lobbying groups. Then, too, it would be a simple matter for the airlines to pay directly into the Treasury. The result would be either that fares would rise quickly and in large amounts, or that the airlines would go back on government subsidy, with the subsequent rise in general income tax.

The nation's air carriers are, in contrast to charges made by private aviation, not big profit makers. Caught in the same growth squeeze as the FAA, the airlines are committed to spending large sums of money just to keep up with passenger demand. Airline income has more than tripled during the past decade. And profits have fallen. The before-tax profit for the scheduled airlines in 1968 was $250 million. In 1967, it had been $350 million.

As airline earnings fall, investor interest dwindles. Airline stocks have been depressed for some time. The Value Line Investment Survey for 1969 rated the airlines in sixty-second place out of a list of sixty-six industrial groups as prospects for investors. Airline stock prices were down about 50 percent in 1968. During the first seven months of 1968, individual line share earnings showed Eastern down to 60 cents from $1.82 in 1967, TWA at 53 cents against $1.70 a year ago, Continental down to 31 cents from 83 cents, and Pan American at 71 cents as opposed to $1.04 in 1967.

As profits dip, expenses soar. The year 1967 found operating expenses up 21.2 percent overall. Costs rose almost that much again in 1968. And the future holds much the same picture. In 1968, United Airlines declined 49.2 percent in earnings. Continental was down 62.5 percent, Eastern 63.3 percent, and TWA, which lost $1.78 million during the first half of 1968, had showed a profit during the same period in 1967 of $7.62 million.

The biggest single cost to the airlines is represented in the purchase of new equipment. The airlines took delivery of 451 new jet aircraft in 1968 at a cost of $2.6 billion. By the end of 1971, outlays for new aircraft will total $7.6 billion. These sums for new equipment, coupled with rising wages (airline pilots have been winning as much as 20 percent increases lately), the costs of delays, advertising and promotion to meet competition, and other factors, present a bleak picture of the airlines' financial capabilities in the years ahead.

The money needed to meet the financial demands of the future must come from somewhere. In the past, the airlines have looked to the large lending institutions for funds to finance new aircraft purchases. But this source may become inaccessible to many lines. James P. Mitchell, a vice-president of the Chase Manhattan Bank, said, in an address given on April 23, 1969, to an air transportation conference in New York, that unless the airlines began to improve their earnings, the money market might be dry to them when seeking funds for new equipment. Mitchell estimated the airlines would need $53 billion between then and 1980 to finance the purchase of new jet planes. He made the point that unless the lines are allowed to earn a respectable profit, they would find growth hindered, if not denied. The CAB allows the airlines to earn a maximum return on investment of 10.5 percent. Only twice in the last decade has the industry managed to exceed this figure. The average return has been between 7 and 8 percent, hardly enough to finance massive programs of new equipment purchases.

Certainly to most citizens the financial woes of the nation's airlines are of little concern. It is difficult for the average citizen to lament profits of $250 million while engrossed in balancing his own checkbook in a time of inflation. But two factors must be kept in mind when weighing the financial health of the nation's airline industry. One is that it has not been long since the lines went off government subsidy. It is in the best interests of every American to see the nation with a healthy, self-supporting airline industry. Any less, and each taxpayer will see more of his money going to support government-run airlines.

The second factor deals with fare structures. Barely 40 percent of the nation's populace has ever flown. Many more would like to. The industry has long studied passenger motivation in an attempt to pinpoint the reasons why most people don't fly. Fear has always been offered as the most likely reason. But more and more, industry studies show that cost, not fear, is playing the prime role in keeping people off airplanes. The industry and government want fares lowered. The CAB determines the fares that may be charged by the airlines on given routes, the determinations being governed by what an airline must receive on each route to show a reasonable profit. With costs spiraling upward, the prognosis for lower fares grows dimmer. Early in 1969, the airline industry was forced to go to the CAB for a fare increase to meet rising costs. It was granted, the boost in fares being set at 3.8 percent across the board. By April of 1969, the lines were readying another request to the CAB for still another fare increase, this one closer to 5 percent. The millions of Americans who would like to partake of air travel in this jet age, but do not because fares are out of their reach, are not likely to fly in the near or even intermediate future.

The nation will have a system of public air transportation. It must, to survive and grow. And this system will be supported by either higher fares or direct government subsidy, each alternative drawing from the purses of the population.

Private aviation's argument that it is the passenger, not the airline, who pays into the Treasury is a misleading and useless argument. As stated earlier, it would be an easy matter for the airlines to pay the 5 percent directly. They would do this by raising fares. No one would win. Either way, it would be the passenger who pays. And sadly, as this book attempts to point out, he would pay without benefit of representation.

Clifton Von Kann, vice-president of the Air Transport Association, addressing a special meeting of the airlines at CAB headquarters on August 13, 1968, stated, "One aspect of the crisis is beyond any question—the impact on the airline passenger. It has been estimated that, in 1967, airline delays cost passengers $50 million in loss of productive time. At this rate, the 1968 losses will amount to several hundred millions of dollars.

"This is a serious loss to the nation in terms of productive manpower alone, but the airlines are more concerned about the personal hardships which their passengers have suffered. For this group, there is no need to elaborate, or to bring out some of the current horror stories. Suffice it to say that civilian and military airline passengers are subjected to terrible dislocations and no other users of the airspace have even begun to share the burdens imposed upon these airline passengers.

"What makes this especially unfair is that the airline passenger provide practically all major airport revenue and are the only users of the airspace who pay their full share of the costs. Los Angeles International Airport received 87 percent of its revenue from the airlines and their passengers last year. They will contribute roughly $250 million this year to the system of airports used by the airlines and a similar amount to the federal government for the use of the airways. Yet this $500 million will buy little for the passengers except overcrowded airports, inefficient airways, and intolerable delays."

In contrast to the amounts paid by airline passengers, private aviation pays only four cents a gallon on the fuel it uses. This applies only to aviation gasoline; it does not include jet fuel, which is not taxed. Of this four cents a gallon, two cents is refunded to the user of the gasoline. The end result is a total contribution to the airways system of two cents on each gallon of gasoline used by private aviation. This amounts to approximately six million dollars a year. And as the number of private aviation jets increases, the contribution decreases, unless offset by increased use of piston aircraft. The use of private jets is especially significant when related to corporate jet aircraft. A corporate jet can fly anywhere, make extensive use of the airways and ATC systems, and pay not a penny for this use. Its fuel is untaxed. It flies free. Its passengers, corporate executives, avoid the airline ticket tax of 5 percent. The aircraft crowds into already overcrowded skies on a first-come, first-served basis with all other aircraft, and is written off by the corporation as a business expense. It is, in the eyes of any corporate accountant, a good deal.

It is necessary, when speaking of government funding and user taxes, to distinguish between the airways system and the airport system. As pointed out earlier in the book, a safe and efficient air transportation system demands coordinated contributions from all segments of the industry. The nation's airports are a crucial part of this system.

In major hub areas, airport facilities are inadequate to handle the flow of traffic in and out of the area, at least under present regulations and modes of operating the ATC system. Still, the FAA has labeled only three geographical areas as "high-density" areas in which measures must be taken to alleviate congestion and insure an adequate safety margin among aircraft. These areas, as might be expected, are New York,

Washington, and Chicago. Affected within these areas are Kennedy, LaGuardia, and Newark airports in New York, O'Hare Airport in Chicago, and Washington National in Washington. It is at these airports that the greatest congestion has occurred, especially during the summer of 1968. The problems of congestion are not, however, limited to these areas alone.

These hub airports, like most other large public airports in the country, were built primarily through the issuance of municipal bonds. The communities served by them maintain and support their upkeep and improvements. Only in the case of Washington National and the recently completed Dulles International Airport in the Washington, D.C., area is the federal government directly involved in airport operations. The FAA operates these two airports in Washington and derives income from their use. In every other case, the airports are owned and operated either by cities, states, or counties, or by private individuals and corporations. It is the responsibility of each community to plan for and execute sufficient airport facilities to meet its own needs.

Generally, this home rule approach to airport construction and operation has worked out with some degree of success. But as the system grows and demands increase, it will become more and more necessary for the federal government to step in, as a source of central planning and funding, to insure airport growth to match national demand. It will become more necessary to develop an integrated airport system, each individual facility linked to the others in some master plan of capability, facility, and performance. It does little good for Los Angeles to develop a superior airport system within its geographical area if aircraft originating there cannot operate at destination airports. There must be compatibility.

At the end of 1966, there were 9,673 airports on record with the FAA. These included 418 heliports and 364 seaplane bases, leaving 8,891 airports to accept fixed-wing, land-equipped aircraft.

In 1967, the number of airports (excluding heliports and

seaplane bases) stood at 9,276. Of these, the airlines serve approximately 830. This number declines each year as local service carriers, or air taxi operators, claim a bigger slice of the route structure pie. However, as the air taxis are assimilated into the category of scheduled airlines, the number of airports served by airlines will undoubtedly go up.

Airports are categorized by the number of enplaned passengers each year. The category "hub" is applied to the busiest airports and areas served. These airports are further broken down into classifications of large, medium, and small. Currently, there are 46 large hubs, 36 medium hubs, and 104 small hubs. These small hub airports, which include such areas as Augusta, Georgia, Amarillo, Texas, Erie, Pennsylvania, and Madison, Wisconsin, seldom see yearly scheduled departures rise above fourteen thousand.

Only 186 airports are busy enough, then, to be rated hub airports. This is not to say that more stringent controls aren't needed at the nation's smaller airports. The midair collisions at Asheville, North Carolina, and Urbana, Ohio, occurred in airport areas in which activity is slight in comparison to other areas of the country. Asheville is categorized by the FAA as a small hub. Urbana isn't even included in the hub category. In the interest of public safety, all aircraft operating in all terminal areas should be under some form of more positive control.

The salient point is that proposals put forth by the DOT and, reluctantly, by the FAA call for restrictions on private aviation operations at only five airports, those mentioned earlier as being centers of the most extreme air congestion. The proposals were made because these largest of the hub areas had become saturated. Lives were in danger. Delays were long and intolerable for millions of citizens. *Something* had to be done until the system could be upgraded to handle traffic flow.

But private aviation refused to accept even temporary restrictions at these five busy areas. It insisted on its rights, as granted under Section 104 of the Federal Aviation Act of 1958, to enter and leave all areas freely and without restraint. And it forecast, with sufficient gloom and foreboding, the destruction of private aviation if restricted at the five problem airports. All this insistence and threatening on the part of private aviation had its effect on the decision makers. Anxious to please, the FAA allocated a certain number of the precious operational slots at the congested airports to private aviation. As a result, the airlines found themselves not only restricted as to hourly operations, but they saw some of those slots given over to private interests. All this has meant less service to the traveling public in those high-density areas.

The federal government has little control over airports. It can, under the federal aid programs to airports, withhold funds from those not measuring up to FAA standards. But this power is seldom invoked, if only because FAA standards for airports are virtually nonexistent. Even exhaustive studies by the FAA fail to provide the agency with guidelines for action, as evidenced by the bird study and resulting approval of the Huntsville jetport. Federal aid to airports is, for the most part, allocated on the basis of political persuasion, just as money for dams, buildings, and public works projects is doled out. The FAA is powerless to direct site selection of new airports or to effect increases in airport capacity. Its only role in airport planning and operation is to provide the necessary air traffic control systems, navigation systems, and runway aids for controlled operations at airports. It does this on a need basis; airports request facilities from the FAA and their requests are weighed against the number of aircraft operations at the facility. Few airports are busy enough to receive this FAA aid.

There are currently 322 airports with FAA-operated air traffic control towers. These airports include all of the hub airports. The role of these hubs in scheduled airline operations is great. Over 95 percent of passenger enplanements are conducted at hub airports. Of this number, over 65 percent of the enplanements occur at the large hubs. It is plain to see why only a few airports fall victim to the squeeze of air congestion.

It is at these few airports that emergency measures have been taken to reduce risk and alleviate delay. Long-term planning will have to consider all airports in concert, but the stopgap measures taken in 1968 were demanded of necessity and crisis.

Airport revenues are generated by the users of the facilities. The airlines pay rent on terminal and hangar buildings, as well as landing fees and miscellaneous handling fees. Passengers contribute through parking lot fees, purchases at concession stands, and, in some cases, by paying a head tax upon departure. Before the severe congestion, most airports proved themselves to be substantial and worthwhile investments, or at least capable of self-sustaining operation. But this was before aviation's growth leaped ahead of all forecasts and mushroomed beyond the bounds of order. This growth has forced the nation's airports to scrabble with the pains of rapid expansion to meet aviation's demands. Kennedy Airport in New York typifies this situation. It cost $60 million to build Kennedy Airport in 1948. Since then, the Port of New York Authority has spent in excess of $400 million to expand and improve the facility. It is still inadequate, the dual result of too rapid growth of the medium it serves and political arrogance on the part of the Port Authority.

The Port of New York Authority (PNYA) is a bistate agency created by the legislatures of New York and New Jersey. One of its functions is to develop and manage the three airports in the New York City area. It has done so with an iron fist, much to the dismay of all segments of aviation. In fact, the PNYA has become the one body in aviation about which all combatants can agree—that it is a power-hungry and profit-hungry dynasty dedicated to enhancing its bondholders' interests at the expense of the traveling public. Individual airlines tread softly when dealing with the PNYA for fear of reprisal from their New York landlord. In October, 1965, ten leading airlines operating in the New York area banded together in the Metropolitan Airlines Committee (MAC) in an attempt to bring leverage against the PNYA in the debate on how to solve New York's aviation ills. Both groups belonged to the Aviation Development Council, a study group formed in the interest of improving aviation in New York. MAC soon dropped out, finding it much too difficult to deal with PNYA within the council. It tried to operate from without, but that, too, proved futile. MAC's failure to make any headway against the PNYA came as a surprise to no one. Even the legislatures of New York and New Jersey, to whom PNYA is responsible, have found themselves impotent when dealing with their creation. The Port Authority overruled both Governor Nelson Rockefeller of New York and Governor Richard Hughes of New Jersey in the matter of a site selection for the area's fourth jetport. Neither state leader fought very hard. The PNYA generates too much revenue for both states to allow it to be criticized openly.

As a result of this hands-off attitude, the PNYA operates as an autonomous agency, running all aviation in the New York metropolitan area without the need to seek counsel or approval from the area's leaders. It has vetoed suggestions that it work in concert with New York City's Transit Authority in developing rapid public transportation between downtown and the airports, a situation that led some critics of the PNYA to remind the public that the transit authority is a nonprofit organization while the PNYA is quite the opposite. Besides, the PNYA collects the tolls on roads and bridges leading from the city, a lucrative source of income. Critics have also pointed to the lack of parking facilities at Kennedy Airport and suggested the PNYA make use of its large parking lot at Aqueduct Raceway, which is directly adjacent to the airport. Revenues from the lease of that lot to Aqueduct are large. The Port Authority has no inclination to give up such a source of revenue for the sake of the convenience of the traveling public.

The federal government has been reluctant to interfere with local aviation matters such as airports. Its participation has been limited to providing the necessary ATC equipment and manpower at those airports that qualify by reason of aircraft activity. And it began offering aid for airport improvements and expansion back in 1946, when the Federal-Aid Airport Program (FAAP) was put into law. Under this plan, which was part of the Federal Airport Act of that year, a yearly National Airport Plan (NAP) was to be prepared in which national needs were to be examined and funds allocated to upgrade those areas considered weak. The CAA administered the plan until the FAA took over its functions. New Programs have been announced and administered each year since 1946 with the exception of 1954, when the entire program was suspended for review.

In considering the federal government's involvement with airports, it is well to consider the fear of many that Washington is taking over some responsibilities that are rightfully the concern of states and cities. No one quarrels with the infusion of federal funds into the sagging airport system in the face of congestion. But the actual operation of airports is another matter, one that cannot be considered without some questioning of the wisdom of such a move on the government's part. It has not occurred as yet, but signs are that unless the individual airport operators and communities begin creative planning and fund raising for airport expansion, the DOT will be left with little choice but to take a more active role in airport affairs.

FAAP applies only to publicly owned airports. Each proposed project must enhance air safety and promote air commerce. FAAP funds have been used for land acquisition, runway construction, taxiways, parking apron construction, and airport lighting. Terminal and hangar construction and general beautifying of airports cannot be accomplished under FAAP. In most cases, FAAP provides 50 percent of the funds needed to do a job, with the local community coming up with the rest.

Since passage of FAAP in 1946, the FAA has directed the payment of $1 billion to airports. In 1967, $1.1 billion was appropriated. The 1968 figure was $1.2 billion. In 1969, the FAAP budget was $70 million. Fiscal 1970 finds it cut to $30 million. Hopefully, the swing to a user-supported system will provide vast new sums of money to be pumped into the airport system. It needs them.

The premise that congestion in the air is caused by a lack of concrete on the ground has given private aviation another peg upon which to hang its argumentative hat. Its spokesmen point to the nation's inadequate airports, especially in major metropolitan areas, and claim that if new and improved private aviation airports were available in these areas, they, the private pilots, would not want to use the larger jetports. Congress, the FAA, CAB, NTSB, and various industry groups have all agreed that more and better airports are the key to easing congestion. But, as pointed out earlier in the book, private aviation has historically condemned such proposals as acts of industry segregation against the smaller planes. Private aviation uses the lack of airports to make points in its general campaign of persuasion. At the same time, it balks at any attempts to put more "reliever" or "satellite" airports into existence. Ideally, every metropolitan area should have its large jetports *and* smaller, all-weather airports for use by private aviation. Swift ground transportation would link airport to airport, and the airports with downtown areas. To date, Minneapolis is the only hub area with a coordinated airport plan that approaches the ideal. There should be more such areas. Perhaps if they were actually available, private aviation would reconsider its objections to making use of them.

Private aviation has also suggested from time to time that shorter runways be constructed alongside major runways at hub airports, on which private planes could operate without interfering with the larger jet aircraft. There is some merit to this suggestion in that it would allow increased utilization of existing facilities. But this increase in activity in itself simply compounds the potential of midair conflict. The existing ATC system in congested areas is not adequate and dependable enough to handle the traffic already present. To begin mixing small, slow aircraft with large, sophisticated airline traffic in parallel landing and takeoff patterns would, in this writer's opinion, increase the probability of midair collision. This probability is even more insured when the mix of highly trained airline pilots and inexperienced private pilots is considered. There is too much conflict in the air now. To increase it any further would be a grave mistake.

Perhaps the greatest stumbling block to quick and effective action by the federal government in solving aviation's ills is the problem's relative lack of importance on the scale of vital government issues. Faced with an unprecedented demand for funding of a myriad of domestic and international programs, the Congress must weigh each request against national needs. Understandably, aviation falls low on the scale. This writer's understanding of such a low priority toward aviation should not be expected of the air traveler stranded for hours as his aircraft circles above destination airports, nor should the family of the victim of a midair collision be expected to weigh the victim's importance against national priorities.

What is needed to persuade Congress to devote more of its energies and funds to aviation is a clarification of issues and an injection of reason into the fray. Perhaps some action on those matters in which large sums of money are not an ingredient would make Congress more willing to allocate larger sums for the correction of the major problems. To impose a no-drinking rule on private pilots would not involve even moderate expenditures of funds. Nor would a general upgrading of pilot training and skills required to operate an aircraft within high-density areas. A gesture on the part of the FAA, no matter how token a one, toward adopting a slightly stronger hand in dealing with private aviation might go a long way in restoring congressional faith in the agency.

No one, this writer very much included, believes that private aviation should be restricted to the point of harm. To my knowledge, no figure in aviation or government has ever called for measures that would prove injurious to private aviation. To the contrary, even the industry's severest critics are quick to acknowledge private aviation's contributions to the nation's economy and the desirability of seeing the industry grow and prosper. Funds allocated for aviation by the federal government must take into account the needs of private aviation, and must be directed toward insuring the growth and prosperity of all of aviation's segments. But until the system that controls aviation in this country is upgraded sufficiently to insure safe and efficient operation of all segments, certain restrictive measures must be taken in the areas of aggravation.

The public, in this case the millions of airline passengers, must be protected from danger imposed by special interest groups. It is the airline passenger who pays most of the bills. It is the airline passenger who has the most to lose. He carries in his bag of credentials a substantial amount of moral right. The contents of the bag might well be used to inject the needed order and reason into what is now a disorderly and unreasonable situation.

CHAPTER SEVEN

A Matter of Climate

Any criticism of private aviation and its role in today's aviation environment must not be leveled only at easily defined problem areas. The drinking pilot and the poorly trained pilot are simple to pinpoint and define. But the case against private aviation is not merely predicated upon two or three major points of conflict. Rather, it must be viewed in relation to the prevailing climate in which all aviation must function.

What is this climate? It is permissiveness on the part of the government regulatory agencies toward the very industries they regulate. It is willingness to bend to the wishes of powerful, self-serving lobbying groups that dedicate themselves to persuasion and control. It is the twisting of facts and misuse of information. It is all these things and more. The end result is the climate of which we speak. And in this climate problems develop, fester, expand, and soon grow out of reach.

Private aviation has found this climate ideal for its goals and ambitions. One need only go back through the files of defeated FAA proposals, many desperately needed in the interest of air safety, to sense just how good the aviation climate has been to private aviation. The air taxi industry, until very recently, has been a good case in point.

Air taxis include both scheduled and nonscheduled operations, with nonscheduled operations the more numerous. Both segments have grown considerably, but the scheduled segment of this industry has led the way in percentage of growth. According to records kept by the FAA, on January 1, 1964, there were 122 FAA-approved scheduled air taxi operators. By October 1, 1967, there were 165 such operators, utilizing 685 aircraft.

Air taxi operators were always considered part of the world of private aviation. As such, they enjoyed the freedom of control inherent in the definition. They were also a valuable addition to private aviation's stable of "mission-oriented segments," as opposed to the casual pilot without mission. But this very mission status, the carriage of passengers for hire, brought about a gradual change in the way the federal government viewed the air taxi industry. Certain individuals in the National Transportation Safety Board questioned the freedom of operation it was given. After all, they reasoned, the scheduled air taxis were doing precisely what the major scheduled airlines were doing. What difference did it make if they were smaller? The mission was the same, and the stakes, passengers' lives, were as high.

This government interest was heightened as the airlines began making increased use of air taxis as extensions of their own service. In this circumstance, an airline would book a passenger from, say, New York to San Francisco and then on to Marysville, California. The passenger would be booked on a California scheduled air taxi flight from San Francisco to Marysville, just as he might be booked on an overseas carrier from San Franciso to Tokyo, all done by the originating airline in New York. Under such arrangements, the passenger was placing the same faith in the air taxi as he was in the major airline that did his booking. It was misplaced faith. By mid-1967, there were 42 contracts between major airlines and scheduled air taxi operators, contracts that allowed a passenger to step from a strictly controlled, modern jet airliner piloted by top professionals into a single-engine private plane, probably with a radio and piloted by anyone meeting minimum standards. This situation caught the attention of officials at NTSB.

At the same time as the NTSB was considering the problems of contracts between airlines and air taxis, another condition came to its attention. This was the increasing use of scheduled air taxis for the carriage of mail. Postmaster General Lawrence F. O'Brien announced early in 1968 that the vast bulk of first-class domestic mail would soon be transported by air. In addition, O'Brien indicated a greater reliance on air taxi operators for such timely movement of the mail. This increase in the use of air taxis by the Post Office Department had already begun to be felt. In 1966, only ten air taxi operators held contracts to carry mail. By the end of 1967, that figure had risen to twenty-nine operators serving 80 mail routes and 240 locations. During 1967, air taxi operators earned $3 million from their mail contracts. The Post Office Department estimated earnings for air taxi operators to be in excess of $8 million in 1968.

Both situations—the increased movement of mail and the increased carriage of airline-originated passengers—provided an interesting comparison for the experts at NTSB. They first took a hard look at the air taxi industry's safety record and found it shocking. This deteriorating record had occurred despite the fact that the air taxi operators, airline contracts aside, were carrying in excess of three million passengers a year. The utilization of air taxis by so many passengers evidently did not impress the FAA enough for it to take any steps to tighten up on air taxi operations. The FAA left them alone, content to see three million people fly on marginal aircraft and with pilots controlled only by the minimal regulations. According to Joseph J. O'Connell, chairman of NTSB, the total number of accidents in air taxi operations increased 15 percent from 1964 to 1965, 13.5 percent from 1965 to 1966, and 7.3 percent from 1966 to 1967. The number of fatal accidents increased 8.7 percent from 1964 to 1965, remained unchanged from 1965 to

1966, and increased 31 percent from 1966 to 1967. The accident rate per 100,000 aircraft hours flown for all accidents, fatal and nonfatal, increased steadily: 10.07 in 1964, 10.65 in 1965, 12.50 in 1966, and 13.25 in 1967.

Even in the face of this, the FAA continued to treat the air taxi industry with the same hands-off attitude it afforded all of private aviation. Had it not been for the Post Office Department, this might still be the case.

The Post Office Department instituted a series of requirements for all air taxi operators bidding for airmail contracts. Among the requirements were stipulations that aircraft carrying the mail must be twin-engine, have complete deicing equipment, be equipped for IFR flight, and be able to operate at the lowest published minimums for airports served. In addition, air taxi pilots carrying mail would have to be IFR-rated, and have a minimum of five hundred flight hours, fifty hours of nighttime operations, and fifty hours of IFR experience under actual weather conditions. These rather stringent requirements went into effect in early 1968.

It didn't take the NTSB long to react to the wide gap between safety regulations imposed by the FAA for air taxis carrying human beings and safety requirements imposed by the Post Office Department for the carriage of mail. In a letter to General William F. McKee of the FAA, dated March 14, 1968, O'Connell addressed himself to the problem, one to which he attached great importance. After citing the obvious facts concerning accident rates for air taxis, mail carriage, and the transportation of passengers, O'Connell made the following point:

"At this point the Post Office Department, with the help of the FAA, is imposing a higher level of safety regulation on air taxi operators carrying *mail* than the Government imposes on the same, or other, air taxi operators who are carrying *passengers* for hire."

O'Connell went on to suggest a number of measures that might be taken to insure a higher level of safety in air taxi operations, including the suggestion to remove air taxis from the private aviation category and place them in the airline category of operations, at least to some degree. To the dismay of private aviation's leading spokesmen, the National Air Taxi Conference welcomed O'Connell's suggestion that the industry be given airline status, regardless of the increased regulatory burden that status would bring.

AOPA, with only a few air taxi operators as members, keenly felt the pending loss of one of its valued segments of private aviation. In the past, AOPA had taken numerous stands in matters relating to air taxis. One in particular concerned a proposed regulation offered by the FAA that would have made the filing of flight plans mandatory for air taxi flights carrying passengers. Flight plan filing is neither complex nor time-consuming. It is simply a matter of filling out a short form on which the pilot indicates his destination, expected route of flight, number of passengers, and estimated time of arrival at the destination. It accomplishes two things. One, of course, is that in the event that flight doesn't arrive at or close to its ETA, an immediate search and rescue operation can be put into effect. Then, too, flight plan filing alerts ground controllers along the flight path to the aircraft's expected entry into their area.

The idea of having air taxis file mandatory flight plans was not a sudden burst of regulatory inspiration within the FAA. The subject had cropped up on numerous occasions in the past, usually following an accident in which S&R efforts took lengthy periods of time to locate the downed aircraft. After every such incident, the idea of mandatory flight plans would be resurrected at the agency. The idea would then be put away following vigorous protests from private aviation, usually led by AOPA. The association would label such attempts infringements on the pilot's rights of freedom and privacy, an unwarranted obligation against the pilot, and a hint of broader regulations to come. AOPA would casually dismiss the safety factors inherent in flight plans, especially where paying passengers were concerned. Its spokesmen would cite those examples of downed aircraft in which a flight plan had been filed and still S&R efforts took longer than expected. It cited all those air taxi flights that hadn't ended in a fatal crash to prove the association's point. It fought for "freedom," and was the victor each time out.

Air taxis, with their millions of passengers, are still not required to file flight plans. Perhaps under their new semi-airline classification these small but vital operations will begin to fall under more rigid and sensible regulation. Hopefully, people will receive the same consideration for their safety as do airmail letters.

It has also been suggested at various times in the past that *all* flights, air taxi and others, operate on flight plans. As it stands, no pilot flying on visual flight rules (VFR) needs a plan of flight. In many cases, especially when such flights are conducted over heavily populated areas, the need for flight plans for search and rescue purposes is slight. This, of course, is not true when flights are conducted over barren areas of the country. Proponents of mandatory flight plans usually cite the S&R reasons for the proposal. But this argument generally falls flat when statistics are unfurled on the number of fatal crashes in which lives were lost as the result of the failure to file a flight plan. Such incidents aren't numerous.

There is, however, the matter of expense, which seldom is introduced into such arguments. The U.S. Air Force spends millions of dollars every year conducting search and rescue missions for lost and downed aircraft. The Civil Air Patrol conducts about half these missions for the Air Force. The other half costs the Air Force, and the taxpayer, over $4,000,000 each year. Much of this could be saved if flight plans were filed prior to flight. Days are spent in search of missing aircraft that have taken off without any notification to anyone of their intended route of flight or destination. Even when flight plans are filed, much wasted S&R work goes on searching for "missing" pilots. In a number of cases, the pilot files a flight plan, arrives at his destination, and fails to close the plan with the Flight

Service office. Hours pass, and the S&R network goes into effect. At times, a simple phone call to the pilot's home will find him comfortably in front of the television. At other times, especially when the destination is not the pilot's hometown, Flight Service cannot locate him. It is assumed he has crashed somewhere between the point of departure and arrival. The Air Force is called in and Civil Air Patrol aircraft scour the area for signs of the wreckage. And all the time, the pilot in question is visiting friends for the weekend. The pilot is not in any way punished or reprimanded for his failure to properly close the flight plan. He can repeat the performance again next weekend.

There is, however, a more valid reason for wanting the filing of flight plans made mandatory. This involves the unannounced intrusion of aircraft into control areas of the country, as occurred in the Urbana tragedy. Arriving suddenly and unexpectedly, these VFR flights that have not had flight plans filed are known as "pop-ups" in the controllers' jargon. The surest way to avoid pop-ups is to have all aircraft under positive control at all times. This is obviously unworkable. The mandatory filing of flight plans is not. It takes perhaps three minutes to file a VFR flight plan. It represents a minimal intrusion into the private pilot's life. It is not a cure-all. But it would help.

Lately, the calls for mandatory flight plans have been replaced by enthusiasm over the use of crash locator beacons aboard aircraft, to facilitate search and rescue operations. Under this proposal, each aircraft would be equipped with an electronic radio beacon that would transmit signals on an assigned frequency to be picked up by searching aircraft. Many prototypes of this device have been tested, ranging in price from under one hundred dollars to over one thousand dollars, the spread determined by the sophistication of the device. In the more expensive models, the beacon would automatically become activated upon a sudden change in the plane's forward motion, as would occur in a crash or forced landing. In the simpler models, the pilot of a downed aircraft would have to activate the device manually, a difficult procedure for an injured airman. In either case, it is generally agreed in the aviation industry that crash locator beacons would be of value in cases of downed aircraft.

But the development of such safety devices raises yet another chapter in the history of private aviation's persecution complex. Convinced that any attempt to make the use of such devices mandatory is little more than the result of pressure from airline interests, private aviation balks at these advances. As with all rule making in the interests of air safety, private aviation champions the concept and vetoes the implementation. Generally, it objections are stated as being born of the cost of the advance. Through its spokesmen, private aviation makes a case for the difficulties of the private pilot in paying for such mandatory devices.

There is another, stronger motivation for this refusal to accept mandatory safety regulations. This involves the broad philosophy that to allow additional regulation over the industry would simply breed more of the same. Consequently, private aviation, typified by the stands of AOPA and applauded by its dues-paying membership, stands firm against such devices as mandatory crash locator beacons in all aircraft. Robert Monroe, AOPA's congressional liaison man, told me he favored crash locator beacons as part of original equipment in all new aircraft, and he further felt they should be a basis for certification by the FAA. But when I asked him if he thought AOPA would be against the mandatory installation of crash locator beacons in existing aircraft, he agreed this would probably be the case. If so, he speculated, it would be based upon displeasure at the wording of the FAA regulation and perhaps on the amount of time given owners of existing aircraft to comply. There is, of course, little sense in determining the worth of a regulation before it is actually offered. But private aviation's history of reluctance to accept new and needed regulations causes the FAA to approach such regulatory proposals with a less than optimistic attitude. The climate of resistance to change has been on the aviation scene for a long time. It is heavy, stifling, and hardly conducive to creative attacks on aviation's problems.

A situation similar to the one involving crash locator beacons exists with electronic devices that function as collision warning systems. Two basic types of these systems are now in development. One, termed PWI (proximity warning indicator), informs the pilot when another aircraft is within unsafe proximity. Having this knowledge and being made further aware of the intruding aircraft's position relative to his aircraft, the pilot can take appropriate corrective actions to avoid collision.

The other type is more advanced. It not only indicates the presence of another aircraft but takes all the necessary evasive action automatically through a computer. There is, however, another level of sophistication that falls between these two categories. This also utilizes a computer, which tells both pilots what evasive action to take as two planes converge. The plane at the lower altitude would be instructed to dive, with an opposite order given the higher plane.

All the devices tested have displayed certain flaws, but the latter conception appears to be most acceptable to the Air Transport Association and the airlines. ATA estimates the cost to run between thirty thousand dollars and fifty thousand dollars per aircraft for the equipment. Some airlines have already budgeted for the installation of this device during 1970. Obviously, the cost of this system is prohibitive for the average small plane owner. And yet, even having all airlines so equipped can insure against collision only between airline aircraft. Those small planes competing in the same airspace would still present a distinct danger of midair conflict. Only the insurance of separation through restriction can be offered as a solution, a suggestion fraught with complications, as evidenced in previous chapters.

Another area contributing to the climate of aviation and benefiting from its smog is the manufacturing of light planes. There is a line of comparison between light plane builders and manufacturers of automobiles. No single segment of private aviation has as much to lose in the fray, at least in a tangible sense, as the Pipers and Cessnas and Mooneys of aviation. These corporations, prospering at impressive rates, have carefully nurtured the growth of private flying. Their stars rise in direct proportion to an increase in the number of citizens taking to the air in their own aircraft. The makers of private planes delivered in excess of $500 million worth of new aircraft in 1968. And FAA forecasts, remarkably conservative in the past, project private plane sales to expand right through the seventies.

Light plane manufacturers have displayed marketing virtuosity in fostering interest in aviation. Cessna led the way with its five-dollar introductory flying lesson, a campaign that has met with huge success and promises more of the same. A general affluence, coupled with increased travel needs of businesses, led private aviation into its growth period of the sixties. But while light plane manufacturers have met the challenge of tapping the nation's personal resources through aggressive and advanced marketing techniques, there remains a serious question as to whether they've met the safety challenges that go with growth. C. O. Miller of NTSB thinks not.

"I am not personally pleased with the stepping up of the safety responsibility that these general aviation manufacturers really could perform. I am not satisfied with this a bit," Miller told me.

QUESTION: Do you mean with the design of aircraft?
MILLER: I am saying that, to a degree, there is an analogous situation to the automobile manufacturers. I think some of the people in the general aviation business have been slow to adopt modern safety engineering principles. We've got an airplane that bothers us right now. If this turns out to be proved, and true, to me it is an unbelievable breach of good safety engineering. It's stuff that other forms of the aviation

business learned years ago. For some reason or other this stuff creeps into general aviation.

QUESTION: What does NTSB do when it discovers a case of design error or faulty safety engineering?

MILLER: The first thing we do is investigate thoroughly and see that we're right. Let's assume we do find a case where a design problem exists in an airplane. We have two ways of going about it. The obvious is to call it to the FAA's attention and ask them to issue some kind of directive requesting correction of the defect. But another way to go about it, and a better way, is through various communications channels—send copies of our public statements to the manufacturers and they will generally take action on their own before the FAA tells them about it. . . . You see, the FAA has a concept of minimums. They don't tell you what to do, but they tell you you must do at least this good for certification. I'm all for this, but I can't say it's worked in the case of general aviation manufacturers. I think the manufacturers' reason is simple. They view themselves in such a tight money situation that they say, by God, we have to cut corners every way we can. It isn't even conscious sometimes.

QUESTION: But it seems they have sufficient money to promote private flying at every turn.

MILLER: Yes. In their view, they have to create more of an interest in flying to have their industry progress at the marketplace. In my judgment, there are safety techniques that manufacturers could use that they haven't used.

QUESTION: What responsibility does the manufacturer of a light plane assume after he's enticed a person to learn to fly? The man finds learning to fly easy, and passing the FAA test even easier. What happens then?

MILLER: I'm interested in the systems safety concept in which everyone has an obligation. But I don't think the manufacturers have looked down the road to see how their product is going to be used. They have an obligation to provide hardware and software to make it work. A good example is the flight manual that comes with airplanes. My car manual is better than most flight manuals I've seen.

QUESTION: What's the FAA's posture in all this?

MILLER: I can look at the FAA and say, why the hell don't you demand more of the manufacturers? But they come back and say their philosophy is minimum standards. One of the problems here is AOPA. If the FAA were to demand a better job on preparing handbooks for new aircraft, AOPA would stand up and say, don't demand things of us. I have never met anyone yet in this business who thought the flight handbooks were adequate.

REPORTER: I was in a pet shop last week in which you had to answer questions before you could buy a dog. They were concerned for the dog's future. It seems, then, it's easier to buy an airplane than a dog.

MILLER: That's a useful analogy in terms of what occurs after the sale is made. The manufacturers will stand back and say that's not our problem. That's a certification problem, they'll claim, and up to the individual pilot once he buys our airplane. I've seen this in some of the manufacturers' statements. I don't buy this.

Despite Miller's personal convictions about light plane manufacturers' lack of concern over the systems concept of safety, the NTSB concentrates its efforts on detecting and suggesting corrections in design flaws. Perhaps the tangible nature of engineering accounts for this emphasis on the hardware, as opposed to manufacturer attitudes and pilot proficiency. There are certainly sufficient cases of design flaws in private aircraft to warrant attention to this area by the NTSB. In fact, NTSB delved deeply enough into the subject to justify the publication of the results of its studies in a bulky report entitled *Aircraft Design-Induced Pilot Error*, issued in July, 1967.

What was especially interesting about this report was that it dealt not with design flaws in themselves, but with how such flaws contributed to pilot error. There has long been a theory advanced that many accidents chalked up to pilot error really resulted from a pilot act brought about by one or more of these design flaws. An example of this might be the placement of the landing gear lever next to, say, the flap activator lever. In such a situation, a pilot could, and has, reached for his flap lever, retracted his landing gear by mistake, and landed wheels up. This would be listed as pilot error by NTSB. But the error was most certainly induced by the placement of the two handles.

The report issued by the NTSB was based on all private aviation accidents in 1964. These accidents were analyzed and categorized by accident type and aircraft model, the specific aircraft designations masked through the use of a numerical code. Some of the designs cited as contributing to pilot error included those dealing with the aircraft fuel system, landing gear design and construction, nosewheel and tail wheel function, warning light function, electrical system capability and function, and always the lack of information contained in aircraft manuals.

In the case of fuel system design, the term fuel mismanagement was applied to all accidents resulting from inadequate fuel reaching the engine, despite the presence of fuel in one or more tanks and a perfectly functioning fuel flow system. In most of these cases of fuel mismanagement, the loss of fuel to the power plant resulted from the pilot's confusion over placement of the fuel flow valves and/or misreading of fuel gauges. It has been pointed out by a number of observers how foolish is the design of aircraft fuel systems in themselves. Only in aircraft is the driver able to run out of gas while the tanks are half filled. Pilots of light aircraft must still remember to switch from one wing tank to another. It often occurs that one tank will run dry and the engine will fail during the lull in fuel flow while the pilot is switching tanks. NTSB also discovered that many cases of fuel mismanagement were caused by the pilot's wrong positioning of the fuel selector during the switchover. In any event, simple conceptual changes in fuel systems could result in a lowering of fuel mismanagement accidents.

Warning lights and audible devices also played a part in NTSB's report. Warning horns to herald an impending stall were so low in volume that the pilot often couldn't hear the horn. Or the stall warning horn would sound identical to the horn that signals when the landing gear is not properly lowered and locked in place. Then, too, failures in aircraft electrical systems sometimes rendered the warning lights and horns useless.

Aircraft flight manuals constantly appeared in NTSB's report as contributing to pilot error. This was especially true for rented aircraft in which the pilot was unfamiliar with the plane's systems and controls, and usually didn't bother to give the manual a thorough reading. Of course, the fact that most aircraft manuals are inadequate to begin with would tend to discount the importance of an aircraft renter skipping through them before flight. Generally, NTSB cited lack of information in the manuals as the problem, although in some cases information contained was actually faulty. Most manuals gave information pertaining only to perfect and normal conditions, never preparing the pilot for abnormal conditions. The manuals cited in this instance gave recommended landing speeds, but only for relatively calm days with dry, moderate weather conditions. Takeoff distances seldom considered weight changes or wet runways. In short, aircraft manuals have been found lacking, not only by most aviation veterans, but by the NTSB. This criticism of light plane flight manuals has seldom prompted the manufacturers to make changes. Only in the case of a distinct error uncovered in a specific manual has the manufacturer gone back to press.

This book does not dwell on the manufacturers of light aircraft for two reasons. One is that it is a subject unto itself, requiring patient technical understanding of the subject. But more important within the conception of this book, design faults in private aircraft do not pose a particularly serious threat to the safety of the nation's millions of airline passengers. These faults generally lead to accidents in which the pilot alone is involved. While this is a serious matter, it would be asking too much for the federal government to spend huge sums of money to protect a few individuals from themselves.

Rather, the role of light aircraft manufacturers in this case against private aviation has to do with their aggressive and shortsighted push to put more people into the air as private pilots. This marketing push has resulted in crowded skies. And too many of the pilots causing this crowding are up there because of the ease with which anyone can obtain his or her private license. Cessna, for a period, intimated in its ads that flying a plane was as easy as driving the family car. That claim has been dropped from the ads, but the feeling prevails.

The aviation medium has become increasingly complex, enough so that there is little room or moral justification for the airborne Sunday driver, especially in larger, more congested areas of the country. The FAA has admitted it can no longer keep pace with aviation's growth, yet this growth rate is actively accelerated through the marketing efforts of the light plane makers. As air traffic increases, it becomes imperative that greater regulation be placed over its flow through the skies. The growth must be matched with reasonable approaches at control, and no lobbying efforts by self-interest groups should hinder the evolution of such control. The free-for-all attitude existing in private aviation is the direct result of too little control and uninhibited fostering of chaotic growth. It is not enough to sell airplanes. With the selling of airplanes must come efforts by the seller to insure a safe system in which the purchaser can operate.

There is little reason to expect the producers of light planes to place self-imposed curbs on their selling and manufacturing efforts. Any curbs must be directed by the one agency with the charter of air safety, the FAA. Not until this agency is able to improve the system of control can aviation continue to absorb, safely, the influx of new planes and pilots.

Dr. Stanley Mohler of the FAA told me a story that is indicative of how much dependence can be placed on the maufacturers' self-control. Safety studies by both NTSB and the FAA have indicated beyond doubt that the use of shoulder harnesses would drastically decrease the number of fatal private aviation injuries. Most deaths resulting from private aircraft accidents occur when the pilot's head strikes the interior of the aircraft. The FAA and NTSB have long advocated the installation of shoulder harnesses in all aircraft. Their suggestions have been met with protests from the industry, the same kinds of protests that accompanied the mandatory placement of seat belts in automobiles. But aircraft manufacturers had one point of defense not available to automobile manufacturers. They claimed that to reinforce the structure of light planes to accept the strain of sudden pulls on shoulder harnesses would cause an overweight problem in the aircraft.

Dr. Mohler, while touring the production line of a leading light plane manufacturer, asked again why the company didn't install the shoulder harnesses, and was given the weight answer. Later, on another production line in the same plant, he noticed new aircraft rolling off with shoulder harnesses installed as original equipment.

"Why do those airplanes have shoulder harnesses?" he asked his guide.

"They're for overseas delivery," the guide answered. "England. They have a regulation over there that every new plane has to have them."

CHAPTER EIGHT

No Easy Answer

Aviation's problem, like all others of magnitude, cannot be solved with easy answers. The individual issues comprising the whole problem are, in themselves, sufficiently complex to demand complex approaches to finding workable solutions. But, as in any problem-solving exercise, priorities must be assigned to the desired end results before anything can be accomplished. There are as many professed goals in aviation as there are interested parties. But one priority must stand above all others. That is an assured reasonable level of safety for the air travelers of this nation. With this goal uppermost in mind, all other goals fall into order of place and need.

To place the safety of the nation's airline passengers in the prime position of priority is not alien to the professed priorities of the federal government. The Federal Aviation Act of 1958 stresses the safety of travelers on public air transportation. And during the 1962 hearings on efficiency and economy in the FAA held by the House Subcommittee of the Committee on Government Operations, Congressman Jack Brooks of Texas stated what millions of airline passengers feel. He was addressing Najeeb Halaby, administrator of the FAA, and said, "We are interested in—I will tell you concisely, Mr. Administrator, what

I am interested in. It is flying safely to Beaumont, Texas, and coming back to see my wife in Washington."

"Right," Halaby answered.

"And everything that can be done to provide that safety, I want the FAA to be doing," Brooks added.

"And that is what we are trying to do, Mr. Brooks."

"And if I can find some evidence that they are not, I am going to get it and present it to you."

"Right," said Halaby.

"I am not trying to embarrass anybody, but I do want to get off that plane after I pay them for riding on it."

"Right."

"I want to be able to walk away."

The simple desire of an airline passenger to walk away from a flight should not be compromised by any efforts of special interest groups. Nor should it become less of a reality through unimaginative and passive rule making by those charged with air safety. It is the right of every citizen to expect that every reasonable effort has been made to insure his safety while a passenger. When he places his confidence in a highly trained and regulated airline pilot, it is reasonable to expect others sharing the airspace to possess compatible qualifications. Other aircraft should be equipped with the basic equipment needed to navigate the airspace safely. The medium is complex and sophisticated, but the need is simple. Safety, above all else.

This book has attempted to point out some of the areas in which private aviation enjoys undue freedom of operation. It has highlighted points of contention between the three partners in air safety—government, airlines, and private aviation. Above all, it has asked that all participants in the aviation debate of the sixties inject reason and a sense of morality into the many arguments that hinder any solutions to the problems themselves.

The following list of recommendations represents the thinking of one man only, the author. There are many approaches to correcting most of aviation's ills. My list includes both those areas needing long-range planning and the infusion of large sums of money and those areas in which change for the better can be accomplished by simple, quick, and independent rule making. In all cases, only the well-being of millions of Americans who fly as passengers on the nation's airlines dictates both the need for change and the approaches to these needs.

1. Establish immediate priorities at all major hub airports at which congestion has occurred to insure safe and expedient passage for the airline passengers using those facilities. If this includes the need to ban private aircraft from large hub airports, either at specified problem hours or under a blanket exclusion, then the appropriate action should be taken. Such a system of priorities should remain in effect until the capacity of these airports and the capability of the air traffic control system serving them has been expanded and improved to insure relatively free and uncongested flow of traffic and adequate separation of aircraft.

2. Immediately formulate a rule change within the FAA that would make drinking before operating an aircraft an offense. The precise number of hours allowed between "bottle and throttle" should be determined by those members of the FAA whose knowledge and experience can best be used for such a determination, the result thereof to be in no way influenced by lobbying organizations or associations affected by such a regulation. It is within the legal and governmental jurisdiction of the FAA to make such rules, despite industry reaction through notices of proposed rule making. Such a regulation would be in the clear interest of all citizens of the United States, and would also be in the interest of all airmen.

3. Establish a true and fair system of funding the aviation system through the user concept, and establish a fair-share formula in which all segments of aviation would pay according to their use of the system.

4. Require the FAA to begin a study of ways to improve the

training of private pilots to reflect more closely the increasing demands of the aviation medium. Such changes should be continuous and aggressive, at least until the number of "pilot error" accidents begins to decrease from year to year.

5. Upgrade the licensing requirements for private pilots, possibly utilizing a classification system based upon the individual's ability and extent of operation. Under such a plan, those pilots holding basic certificates would not be allowed to operate aircraft in areas in which more stringent requirements are necessary. For an airman to enter a highly congested area, he would be required to hold an advanced airman's certificate, which has been obtained after more rigorous training and testing.

6. Establish a program of recertification under which all airmen would be required to demonstrate their skills and knowledge at predetermined intervals. Any increased costs to the FAA for conducting such a program would be borne by the individual, just as the periodic renewing of driver's licenses is accompanied by a fee.

7. Limit, if necessary, the output of new aircraft and the issuance of new private pilot's certificates until such time as the FAA is able to close the gap between its powers of regulation and the industry to be regulated.

8. Recognize the need for more air traffic controllers and conduct a vigorous campaign of recruitment and training.

9. Begin to put more of the responsibility for the testing of private pilots, and the certification of mechanical work performed on aircraft, back into its proper place, the FAA.

10. Develop a strong central planning agency for airport development, and begin funding an accelerated program of airport modernization, expansion, and utilization. Begin building more and better airports in metropolitan areas for the use of private aircraft.

11. Elevate the FAA and its body of experts to a plateau above the reach of self-serving industry groups, a plateau from which decisions can be made in the interest of public safety only.

12. Reevaluate the Federal Aviation Act of 1958 in relation to the growth of the aviation medium.

13. Establish a vocal and active airline passenger association to balance the power of such private aviation groups as AOPA. Until decisions can be made by law and rule makers free of the influence of industry groups, it is imperative that all sides have equal representation.

GLOSSARY

GLOSSARY OF AVIATION TERMS

AERIAL APPLICATION The discharge of materials from an aircraft in flight. Commonly refers to agricultural activity such as crop-dusting.

AEROBATICS The performance of stunts in an aircraft, such as steep banks, dives, loops, rolls, etc.

AERONAUTIC CHART Map of portions of the earth's land areas used by pilots in aerial navigation.

AILERON Control surface located on the aircraft's wings. Manipulation of these surfaces by the pilot results in a change in the aircraft's movements. As he turns the control wheel in the cockpit to the left, the plane will lower its left wing and begin turning in that direction. The same applies to a right-hand movement.

AIR CARGO All commercial air express and air freight, but not including airmail and air parcel post.

AIRCRAFT ACCIDENT (INCIDENT TO FLIGHT) An aircraft accident occurring between the time an engine or engines are started for the purpose of commencing a flight and the aircraft comes to rest with all engines stopped.

AIRCRAFT CONTACTED Aircraft with which FAA flight stations have established radio contact.

AIRCRAFT OPERATION Used as a statistical measure by the FAA. Each aircraft arriving at or departing from an airport with an FAA airport traffic control service is counted as one aircraft operation. There are two types of such operations: local and itinerant. Local operations are those that operate in the local traffic pattern or within sight of the tower, or those known to be departing for or arriving from flight practice areas located within a twenty-mile radius of the control tower. Itinerant operations are all aircraft arrivals and departures other than local operations.

AIR LANE A route in the air, usually controlled by FAA ground control facilities and possessing certain air navigation aids.

AIRMAN A pilot, mechanic, or other licensed aviation technician.

AIRMAN CERTIFICATE In effect, a license certifying the airman to perform certain acts or services. Such licenses (pilot, mechanic, instructor, etc.) are issued by the FAA.

AIR POCKET An occurrence in the air in which sudden downward or upward drafts of air will cause an aircraft to drop, swerve, or rise suddenly and unexpectedly.

AIRPORT An area of land or water that is used or intended to be used for the landing and takeoff of aircraft, and includes any buildings and facilities.

AIRPORT ADVISORY Referred to as AD. ADs are information given to arriving or departing aircraft concerning wind, runway in use, altimeter setting, other known traffic in the area, and airport conditions.

AIRPORT BEACON A rotating beacon located at or near an airport to indicate either the specific or general location of the airport.

AIRPORT SURVEILLANCE RADAR (ASR) A short-range radar used by airport traffic control within a thirty-mile radius of the airport.

AIRPORT TRAFFIC Aircraft operating in the air or on an airport surface, exclusive of loading ramps and parking areas.

AIRPORT TRAFFIC CONTROL SERVICE Air traffic control service provided by an airport traffic control tower for aircraft operating on surface areas or in the vicinity of the airport.

AIRPORT TRAFFIC CONTROL TOWER (TOWER) A raised facility operated by the FAA to promote the safe, orderly, and expeditious flow of air traffic at the airport.

AIRPORT TYPE *General Use:* Airports serving as regular, alternate, or provisional stops for scheduled and large irregular air carriers; non-air carrier airports offering a minimum of services, such as fuel and regular attendants during normal working hours; and airports operating seasonally that qualify under above definition. *Limited use:* Airports available to the public but not equipped to offer minimum services. *Restricted Use:* Use by general public prohibited except in case of a forced landing or by previous agreement.

AIR ROUTE Same as Air Lane.

AIR ROUTE TRAFFIC CONTROL CENTER (ARTCC) An FAA facility established to provide air traffic control service to flights operating on instrument flight rules (IFR) within controlled airspace, particularly during the en route phase of the flight.

AIRSPEED The speed of an aircraft in flight in relation to the air through which it flies.

AIRSPEED INDICATOR The instrument in the aircraft that tells the pilot his airspeed.

AIR TRAFFIC Aircraft in operation anywhere in the airspace or moving on land surfaces within airport boundaries.

AIR TRAFFIC CLEARANCE Clearance given an aircraft to operate within controlled airspace.

AIR TRAFFIC CONTROL (ATC) The control of air traffic to insure the orderly and safe flow of such traffic. This term is also used to denote the service or organization controlling the air traffic.

AIR TRAFFIC CONTROL SPECIALIST (CONTROLLER) The duly authorized person charged with air traffic control.

AIR TRAFFIC HUB Not an airport, but a city or area requiring aviation services. Communities fall into four classes as determined by their percentage of the total enplaned passengers in scheduled service of the fixed-wing operations of the domestic certified route air carriers (airlines) in the forty-eight contiguous states and District of Columbia.

AIRWAY A designated air route between points on the earth's surface; specifically, a civil airway.

AIRWAY BEACON A rotating beacon located on or near an airway, as opposed to airport beacons located near an airport.

AIRWORTHINESS CERTIFICATE A certificate issued by the FAA signifying that an aircraft conforms to the type design (except for the experimental classification) and is in condition for safe operation.

ALTIMETER An instrument located in the pilot's cabin to measure the plane's altitude.

ALTIMETER SETTING Adjustment the pilot must make in his altimeter as he encounters different airports. Since each airport differs in its elevation above sea level, the plane's altimeter must be adjusted accordingly to avoid erroneous readings.

APPROACH The maneuvers leading up to the landing.

APPROACH CONTROL The control of aircraft either arriving at, departing from, or flying in the vicinity of a controlled airport. All flights under such control are flying IFR.

APPROACH PATTERN The maneuvers taken by an aircraft while preparing to land. Also called a Landing Pattern.

APRON The area at an airport on which aircraft are parked.

AREA POSITIVE CONTROL Control over designated areas where special air traffic control rules prescribed by the FAA are applicable.

AUTOMATIC DIRECTION FINDER An electronic navigation aid in aircraft that allows the pilot to tune to a ground radio transmitting station, and automatically indicates to the pilot the exact direction of the station from the plane. Also called a Radio Compass.

BANK The attitude of an aircraft in which one wing is lowered.

CAB Civil Aeronautics Board.

CEILING The maximum height at which an aircraft can perform effectively under given conditions. Also a determination of weather; clouds, dust, or smog can constitute a ceiling. Routinely used to refer to the lower limits of a cloud overcast.

CHECKLIST Lists carried in aircraft to aid pilots in remembering procedures for takeoffs, landings, and in-flight operations.

CHECKOUT Testing a person or piece of equipment to ascertain his or its proficiency and capability. Check Flight is a flight conducted to test a pilot or plane.

CIRCLE MARKER A circular band or mark at the center of a landing area or at the point where runaways intersect.

CIVIL AIRWAY An airway designated by the appropriate civil authority for use in domestic and foreign air operations.

CLEARANCE An authorization, verbal or written, for an aircraft to depart from an airport and/or to fly a given route. Also used to designate the form commonly used to grant such clearances.

CLIMB-OUT The climb made by an aircraft directly after takeoff.

COCKPIT CHECK An inspection of all instruments in the cockpit prior to takeoff.

COLLISION COURSE The course taken by an aircraft that will result in a mid-air collision unless some deviation is made.

COMBINED STATION/TOWER A combined facility in which an Airport Traffic Control Tower and a Flight Service Station function together.

CONTROL AREA (CONTROLLED AIRSPACE) Airspace of given dimensions in which aircraft operate under Air Traffic Control.

CONTROL TOWER An elevated structure at airports from which arriving and departing aircraft are controlled. These towers are constructed and staffed by the FAA.

CONTROL ZONE An airspace with clearly defined dimensions extending up from the ground surface and including one or more airports in its confines. Air Traffic Control rules, in addition to those covering Control Areas, are in effect.

CROSS-COUNTRY (FLIGHT) A flight of some duration that takes the aircraft and pilot away from the immediate vicinity of the airport of departure. This usually involves the landing of the aircraft at airports other than the airport of departure.

CRUISE SPEED The speed at which an aircraft cruises in straight and level flight. It will vary due to wind and weather conditions. Altitude also plays a part.

DANGER AREA An area in which invisible flight hazards exist; can be flown through or over only with proper authority.

DIVE Nose-down descent of an aircraft.

DUAL INSTRUCTION An instruction situation in which the student pilots the aircraft using a second set of controls.

ELEVATION The height or altitude of an aircraft above the earth's surface or above another aircraft.

ELEVATOR A control surface on an aircraft used to control up and down movement. By pulling back on the control wheel or stick, the pilot causes the elevator to move on the plane's tail, sending the aircraft's nose up in the air. Also used to effect the slowing down of an aircraft; the raised nose causes a decrease in speed. An opposite movement produces opposite aircraft movements.

ELIGIBLE AIRCRAFT An aircraft with a current Airworthiness Certificate that, through a periodic or progressive inspection, has been renewed within the past twelve months.

EN ROUTE AIR TRAFFIC CONTROL SERVICE Air traffic control service provided IFR flights as they proceed between two terminal areas.

ESTIMATED TIME OF ARRIVAL (ETA) The predicted and plotted time an aircraft will reach its destination.

FAA Federal Aviation Administration.

FAS Flight Advisory Service.

FEDERAL AIRWAY A path through the navigable airspace of the United States designated by the FAA as suitable for interstate, overseas, or foreign aviation operations.

FINAL APPROACH (FINAL) The final leg of the landing pattern for aircraft; when the aircraft is lined up with the runway.

FIXED-GEAR AIRCRAFT An aircraft with landing gear that remains extended through all phases of flight.

FIXED-WING AIRCRAFT Aircraft having its wings fixed to the fuselage and remaining outspread in flight, as opposed to helicopter-type aircraft.

FLAP A control surface usually located at the rear edge of the wing which, when manipulated by the pilot, changes the wing's characteristics and causes increased lift.

FLAT SPIN A flight situation in which the aircraft spins on its vertical axis in a flat and level attitude. Especially dangerous at low altitudes. More normal spins, equally as dangerous, occur with the aircraft in a nose-down position.

FLIGHT ADVISORY SERVICE (FAS) Advice and information provided by a flight center to assist pilots in the safe conduct of their flights. Provided by the FAA.

FLIGHT ASSISTANCE SERVICE An FAA assistance and advisory service to help pilots in the safe completion of their flights.

FLIGHT CHARACTERISTIC A characteristic peculiar to an aircraft or type of aircraft while in flight; e.g., tendency to spin, yaw, or stall.

FLIGHT CHECK A flight conducted to ascertain pilot proficiency or the capability or performance of an aircraft.

FLIGHT PLAN Specified information given orally or in writing by the pilot of an intended flight to the FAA Air Traffic Control Center at point of the flight's origin. A flight plan must be filed prior to departing for all flights under Instrument Flight Rules (IFR). It is not mandatory to file under Visual Flight Rules (VFR), although the FAA recommends that flight plans be filed for all flights.

FLIGHT SERVICE STATION (FSS) A facility operated by the FAA to render flight assistance.

FLIGHT SIMULATOR A training device used to train pilots. It is mounted on the ground, and the pilot inside performs procedures as the simulator creates flight conditions.

FLIGHT TIME Time spent by a pilot in actual operation of an aircraft.

FORCED LANDING An unplanned landing brought about by such things as adverse weather conditions, equipment failure, etc.

FSS Flight Service Station.

FUEL CONSUMPTION The amount of aviation fuel consumed in gallons or pounds per hour.

FUEL RESERVE An amount of fuel carried in excess of what has been estimated as sufficient to conduct a given flight.

FUEL SELECTOR Switch that enables the pilot to draw fuel from either of the two fuel tanks carried by most aircraft.

GCA Ground Control Approach.

GLIDE A descent by an aircraft in which little or no engine power is utilized, the descent is maintained by the force of gravity, and the speed of vertical descent is controlled by the lift forces on the aircraft.

GLIDE PATH The path through the air of an aircraft in a glide. Also used to denote the path of an aircraft landing in an instrument landing system, the path directed by a radio beam from the ground.

GLIDER An aircraft without a power source that remains in the air because of the natural lift forces acting upon oversized wings.

GROUND CONTROL APPROACH (GCA) An instrument landing system in which the pilot is continually informed of his position and direction by radio contact with the GCA operator at the airport. The operator determines the aircraft position through the use of his radar. The system is used in poor weather conditions.

GROUND SCHOOL Classes conducted as part of a pilot's training. Subjects are nonflying in nature and cover areas related to the total flying picture.

HELIPORT Any surface approved by the FAA for the operation of helicopter aircraft, including rooftops and water.

HOLD A specified point at which aircraft circle while waiting for clearances to proceed to a landing or to another route of flight.

IFR Instrument Flight Rules.

IFR AIRCRAFT HANDLED An FAA statistical measure arrived at by multiplying by two the number of IFR departures from a given location (the assumption being that every IFR departure will have an IFR arrival at another point) and adding the number of IFR flights passing over or through the area.

IFR CONDITIONS Weather conditions below those allowing Visual Flight Rules operations.

ILS Instrument Landing System.

INITIAL APPROACH The holding pattern or course flown by an aircraft just prior to making the final approach to the runway. Usually applies to flight under IFR conditions.

INSTRUMENT APPROACH A landing approach made without any visual reference to the ground and by using instruments and/or radio contact for guidance.

INSTRUMENT FLIGHT RULES (IFR) Rules governing operations in which the pilot depends on his instruments for orientation and navigation. Such flight becomes mandatory in poor weather conditions. An appropriate pilot's rating must be held in order to fly IFR.

INSTRUMENT LANDING SYSTEM A radio guidance system used under conditions of low or no visibility that guides an aircraft down to a landing by means of directional radio beams and radio marker beacons along the approach path.

INSTRUMENT RATING The license authorizing a pilot to operate an aircraft under Instrument Flight Rules.

LANDING ROLL OR RUN The natural, unpowered movement of an aircraft after it has landed.

LANDING SPEED The stated minimum speed at which an aircraft may land and still be under control.

LARGE AIR TRAFFIC HUB A community having 1 percent or more of the total enplaned passengers in scheduled service of the fixed-wing operations of the airlines in the forty-eight contiguous states and the District of Columbia.

LETDOWN The gradual descent of an aircraft from cruising altitude to a lower altitude, usually prior to a landing.

LINK TRAINER A type of ground simulator used for pilot training.

LOG A record book in which is entered either the operational history of a particular aircraft or the flying hours of a pilot.

MEDIUM AIR TRAFFIC HUB A community having from 0.25 to 0.99 percent of the total enplaned passengers in scheduled service of the fixed-wing operations of the airlines in the forty-eight contiguous states and the District of Columbia.

MINIMUM The lowest limit of ceiling, visibility, or altitude at which flight operation is permitted.

NAFEC National Aviation Facilities Experimental Center of the FAA, located in Atlantic City, New Jersey.

NAVIGABLE AIRSPACE The airspace located above minimum altitudes prescribed as safe in which air navigation is permitted.

NONHUB A community having less than 0.05 percent of the total enplaned passengers in scheduled service of the fixed-wing operations of the airlines in the forty-eight contiguous states and the District of Columbia.

NUMBER OF PLACES The minimum crew of an aircraft plus the maximum number of passenger seats. Used in various FAA statistical studies.

OPERATIONS The center at larger airports that directs flying operations.

PANEL The board in an airplane cockpit holding the various flight instruments.

PASS A brief flight over a target or landmark; a run or pass over the mark.

PATTERN The combination of flight paths flown by an aircraft when near an airport as it prepares to land or as it leaves the airport area after takeoff.

PILOTAGE Navigating by visual reference to the ground and its landmarks. Also termed Piloting.

PILOT BRIEF Information furnished a pilot upon which he can plan his flight. Includes weather, airport conditions at destination, routes, wind conditions, etc.

PILOT CERTIFICATE The license granted by the FAA that allows its recipient to operate an aircraft of the type specified on the license and under conditions covered in his certification.

PISTON AIRCRAFT Aircraft powered by engines in which pistons move back and forth to turn the propellers.

PLACARD A posted notice on aircraft stating certain requirements or limits for that particular aircraft.

POWER SETTING The setting of the controls that regulate the amount of power from the aircraft's engines.

PREFLIGHT Preparations before actually conducting a flight. Also refers to ground school preparation of a student pilot for his actual flight training.

PRIVATELY OWNED AIRPORT An airport that is owned by a private individual or corporation.

PRIVATE USE AIRPORT An airport that is not open for the general public.

PUBLICLY OWNED AIRPORT An airport that is owned by a city, county, state, or the federal government.

PUBLIC USE AIRPORT An airport that is open for the use of the general public.

RADAR The use of transmitted, reflected, and timed radio wave signals for tracking objects. The prime tool in the Air Traffic Control system.

RADIO AID Any navigation aid in which a radio plays a part.

RADIO NAVIGATION Navigation using any of the radio-oriented systems.

REGISTERED AIRCRAFT Aircraft registered with the FAA.

REPORTING POINT A geographical location serving as a point of position for an aircraft.

REVENUE Income to air carriers for services performed.

REVENUE AIRCRAFT DEPARTURES An FAA statistical measure consisting of all airline aircraft takeoffs actually performed for revenue.

REVENUE AIRCRAFT MILES The total airline miles flown in revenue service.

REVENUE HOURS FLOWN The actual hours flown by airlines on revenue-producing flights. Such hours are computed from the moment an aircraft leaves the ground until it touches down again at the end of the flight.

REVENUE LOAD CAPACITY The average overall carrying capacity (tons) offered for sale by aircraft in revenue service, including passengers and allowable passenger baggage.

REVENUE PASSENGER A person paying for and receiving air transportation from an airline. Airline employees flying at discount rates and infants charged token fares are not included in this statistical figure.

REVENUE PASSENGER ENPLANEMENTS The total number of revenue passengers boarding aircraft in any given period of time.

REVENUE PASSENGER MILE One revenue passenger transported one mile in revenue service.

REVENUE TON MILE One ton of revenue traffic transported one mile.

ROLL The rotation of an aircraft around its longitudinal axis.

ROTORCRAFT A helicopter.

RUN-UP Racing the aircraft engine for the purposes of testing its performance prior to flight.

SAFETY BELT Same as a seat belt in a car.

SCHEDULED OPERATION Flights conducted by an airline over its certified routes and based upon its published flight schedules.

SECONDARY AIRPORT An airport designated as a satellite receiving airport for aircraft when the primary airport is not available.

SHOULDER HARNESS Restraining straps from an aircraft's interior roof that go over the pilot's shoulders. The same as a shoulder harness in an automobile.

SINK Descending in flight.

SMALL AIR TRAFFIC HUB A community having from 0.05 to 0.24 percent of total enplaned passengers in scheduled service of the fixed-wing operations of the airlines in the contiguous forty-eight states and the District of Columbia.

SOLO FLIGHT (SOLO) A flight in which the pilot is alone in the aircraft.

SPIN A maneuver of an aircraft, planned or accidental, in which the aircraft descends in a corkscrew pattern, its lift lost due to a high angle of the nose.

SPIRAL A corkscrew ascent or descent in which lift has not been lost and the pilot is in control of the aircraft.

STALL A condition in which the nose of the aircraft is raised sufficiently to cause the wings to lose their ability to maintain lift for the plane. Each aircraft has a certain airspeed at which a stall will occur.

STALLING ANGLE The angle at which a given wing will stall as it moves through the air.

STALLING SPEED The airspeed at which an aircraft will stall.

SUPERSONIC TRANSPORT AIRCRAFT A transport plane capable of flying faster than the speed of sound, i.e., faster than 760 mph at sea level in standard atmosphere, or faster than 660 mph at an altitude of forty thousand feet.

TAB A small surface attached to the trailing edge of a horizontal surface (wings, etc.) that, when activated, makes small corrections in aircraft movement and aids in the movement of the larger surfaces.

TAKEOFF DISTANCE The distance required for a given aircraft under given weight conditions to take off.

TAKEOFF RUN OR ROLL The time from when the aircraft first begins to move down a runway until it lifts off the ground.

TAKEOFF SPEED The speed at which a given aircraft will lift off the ground under certain conditions.

TAKEOFF TIME The time at which a takeoff is scheduled or actually accomplished.

TAXI All aircraft movement on the ground while under its own power, except for takeoff and landing rolls.

TERMINAL AREA TRAFFIC CONTROL FACILITY An Air Traffic Control Tower providing service to incoming and outgoing IFR flights, and occasionally en route control service.

TOUCHDOWN The point of contact between the landing gear and the surface of the earth or water.

TRAFFIC PATTERN The prescribed pattern of flight for aircraft when in the vicinity of an airport.

TRICYCLE LANDING GEAR Landing gear consisting of a wheel under each wing (or on each side of the fuselage) and a wheel under the nose of the plane.

TURBINE-POWERED AIRCRAFT Jet-powered aircraft.

TURBOJET Pure jet aircraft. Movement is accomplished by the force of air pushed from the rear of the engines.

TURBOPROP Engine in which a propeller is turned as the result of jet power.

UNDERSHOOT Falling short of the intended landing spot.

VFR Visual Flight Rules.

VISIBILITY The horizontal distance over which good vision is possible.

VISUAL FLIGHT Flight in which the pilot depends on his vision, not instruments, to determine his altitude, route, attitude, etc.

VISUAL FLIGHT RULES (VFR) Rules determining minimum weather conditions for the conduct of Visual Flight. In most areas, it requires three miles forward visibility and one-thousand-foot ceiling above.

ZERO ZERO A weather condition in which there is neither horizontal nor vertical visibility.